H. Harris. del.

Station Grand Junction_Railway, Vauxhall, Birmingham.

Published by J. Drake, Birmingham.

DEDICATED BY PERMISSION TO THE CHAIRMAN AND DIRECTORS OF THE GRAND JUNCTION RAILWAY COMPANY.

DRAKE'S

ROAD BOOK

OF THE

GRAND JUNCTION RAILWAY

FROM

BIRMINGHAM TO LIVERPOOL AND MANCHESTER,

ILLUSTRATED BY AN

ACCURATE MAP, AND NUMEROUS ENGRAVINGS:

To which is appended

THE VISITER'S GUIDE

TO

BIRMINGHAM, LIVERPOOL, AND MANCHESTER.

A Reprint

MOORLAND REPRINTS

2nd edition originally published 1838
This edition published 1974

ISBN 0 903485 25 7

Printed in Great Britain by
The Scolar Press Ltd.,
59/61 East Parade, Ilkley, Yorkshire

for the Publishers
Moorland Publishing Company,
The Market Place, Hartington, Buxton, Derbyshire

TO THE

CHAIRMAN AND DIRECTORS

OF THE

GRAND JUNCTION RAILWAY COMPANY,

THIS

Second Edition

OF

THE ROAD BOOK,

IS,

BY PERMISSION, RESPECTFULLY INSCRIBED,

BY THE

AUTHOR AND PUBLISHER.

ADVERTISEMENT

TO THE

SECOND EDITION.

The courteous reception given to the First Edition of the Grand Junction Road Book, and the substantial proofs of approbation which a rapid sale has afforded, render it a duty as proper as it is pleasant, for the Author and Publisher to return their joint thanks for the liberal patronage already bestowed on their work; and to engage a continuance of the same, by their assurances that in the present edition every possible improvement has been carefully effected in its various departments. Spirited wood and steel engravings * of the most important spots on the line have been introduced, and much new and interesting matter supplied. The whole of the information concerning fares, regulations, stations,

* The work is published either with or without the steel plates.

and accommodation in towns on the route, has been re-cast, corrected, and enlarged; and a brief but comprehensive directory added, under the head of "VISITER'S GUIDE," page 97, containing lists of public buildings; institutions of all kinds; places of worship of all denominations, with names of the officiating ministers; principal show rooms and manufactories; times of arrival and departure of mails at the post office; hackney coach fares; bankers, inns, boarding houses, omnibus offices, newspapers, canal conveyances, waggon warehouses, packets, &c., &c., for Birmingham, Manchester, and Liverpool. The exceeding utility of this new division of the volume will be obvious to every one. The Map has also been revised, and greatly improved; and the "GRAND JUNCTION ROAD BOOK" again makes its bow to the public, in full expectation that its old fame and new merits will be rightly appreciated.

Birmingham, September 1, 1838.

SONNET

BY WORDSWORTH,

ON

STEAM BOATS, VIADUCTS, AND RAILWAYS.

MOTIONS and means, on land and sea at war
With old poetic feeling; not for this,
Shall ye, by Poets even, be judged amiss!
Nor shall your presence, howsoe'er it mar
The loveliness of nature, prove a bar
To the mind's gaining that prophetic sense
Of future change that point of vision, whence
May be discover d what in soul ye are.
In spite of all that beauty may disown
In your harsh features, Nature doth embrace
Her lawful offspring in Man's art; and Time,
Pleased with your triumphs o'er his brother Space,
Accepts from your bold hands the proffer'd crown
Of hope, and smiles on you with cheer sublime.

DRAKE'S MAP OF THE GRAND JUNCTION RAILWAY.

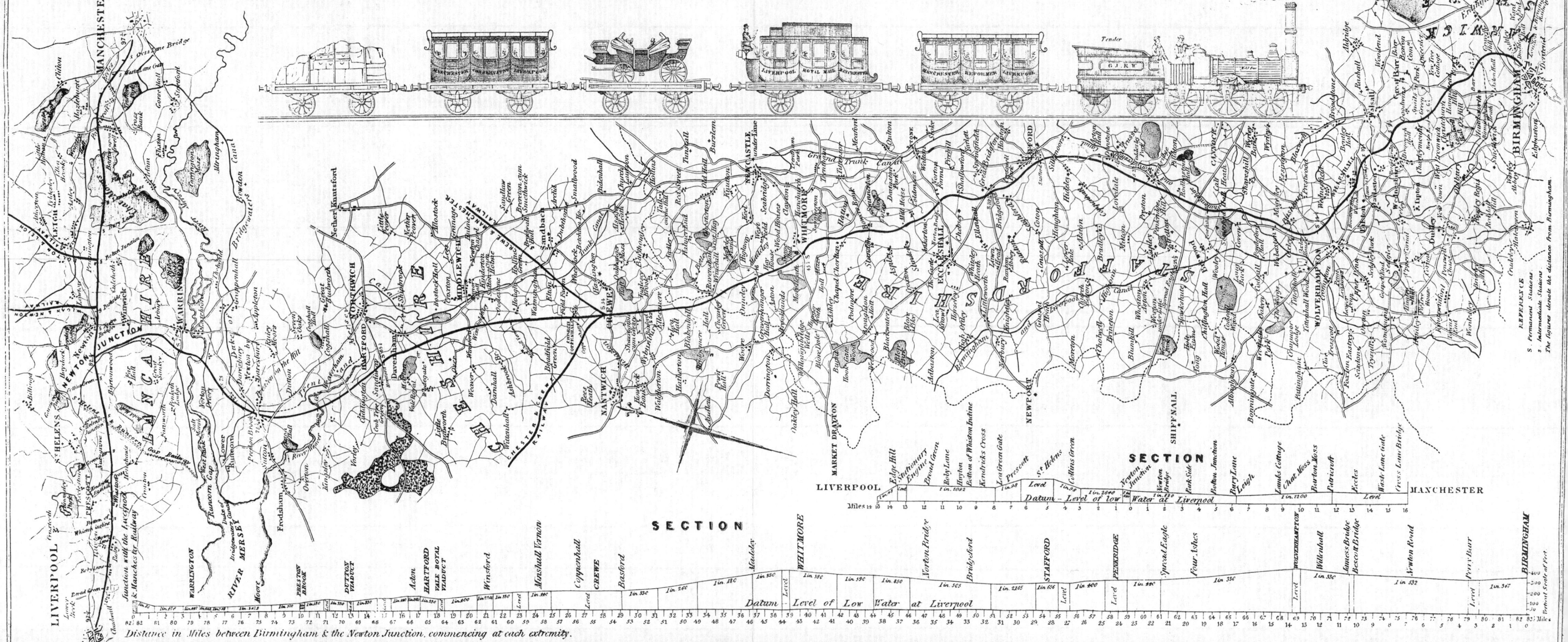

Published by J. Drake, 52, New Street, Birmingham.—Longman & Co. and Hayward & Moore, Paternoster Row, and Simpkin & Marshall, Stationers Court, London.

CHAPTER I.

BIRMINGHAM.

NAME — HISTORY — MANUFACTURES — PUBLIC BUILDINGS AND INSTITUTIONS, &c., &c.

OUR native town of BIRMINGHAM, of whose celebrity and importance we are justly proud, demands our first attention in this our Itinerary; although the numerous publications which give more circumstantial particulars respecting it than the brief limits of the present work will admit, render it an unnecessary task here to occupy many pages with our notice.

In our after topography and history of towns on the "Grand Junction" line, we shall have occasion to allude to their several claims to the honours of "hoar antiquity;" but none it would appear can boast of more remote fame than our own brave old town of Birmingham, or, as it has been variously written, *Bromycham*, *Bremecham*, *Bermyngham*, and *Bromwycham*, the etymology of which terms have served to puzzle the learned in such lore for years gone by, and will do for years to come. What never can be positively settled, always proves a most fascinating subject for argument. Mr. Hutton, the antiquary, imagines the derivation to be this: *wich*, or *wick*, being used to signify a town or village, and *brom*, from the *broom* growing in the vicinity. But we must leave the subject for more voluminous writers. The late Mr. Hamper, our especial antiquary, traced the orthography through no less than *one hundred and forty* variations. In proof of Birmingham being a place of no very recent creation, the prodigious accumulation of scoria produced by the smelting of iron, at Aston furnace, may be referred to; as also the great number of exhausted coal mines, on a large common within a few miles, called Wednesbury Old Field. Both these must have been the work of many centuries, as is proved by the fact, that in the former, the mass of scoria has not perceptibly increased within the memory of that remarkable individual, "the oldest inhabitant," though constantly receiving additions. It appears that the Britons were acquainted with the use and manufacture of iron previously to the Roman conquest, as they are described with chariots armed with scythes. It requires no very great stretch of imagination to suppose Birmingham (the *Bremenium* of the Romans) to have been a chief station for the fabrication of such weapons. In Doomsday Book, "*Bermengeham*" is noticed; and the manor and lordship were held by the De Birmingham family and their ancestors, during the reigns from Henry I. to Henry VIII., when John Dudley, afterwards Duke of Northumberland, being in possession of Dudley, and desirous of adding to it the manor of Birmingham, contrived, by a series of villanous artifices and perjury, to wrest it from Edward de Birmingham, and add it to his own possessions. On the attainder and execution of the duke, in the reign of Mary, the manor escheated to the crown; and in 1643 a descendant of the family, through the female line, was raised to the peerage, by the title of Baron Ward, of Birmingham, changed afterwards to Viscount Dudley and Ward, and Earl of Dudley. The remains of the ancient manor house have long been removed to make way for improvements; its former name, "The Moat," (now called Smithfield,) and two neglected effigies in St. Martin's church, of a crusader and an ecclesiastic of the De Birmingham family, are all that remain to tell of their former greatness. Few historical events seem to have disturbed the good people of Birmingham except the civil war of the seventeenth century, when they proved themselves staunch adherents to the parliamentarians, and did good service to their partizans, against Prince Rupert and his troops, at which time some earth works thrown up at Bordesley, conferred the name of Camp Hill on a part of it. The prince afterwards set fire to the town, but obligingly desisted from further demonstration of such warm regard, on being handsomely bribed to that effect. The riots of 1791 are so frequently brought to the minds of our town's people by present allusions, that it needs not to dwell here on the disgraceful theme. Turning to a pleasanter topic, we will briefly glance at the manufactures which made an anonymous poet formerly exclaim,—

> "Europe's grand toy-shop, art's exhaustless mine—
> These, and more titles, Birmingham, are thine."

It is amusing to look back to the condition of Birmingham in Leland's time, (Henry VIII.,) who describes it as inhabited only "by smithes that use to make knives and all manner of cutting tools, and lorimers that make bittes, and a great many nailors." Camden, in the reign of Elizabeth, speaks of it as "swarming with inhabitants, and echoing with the noise of anvils; but the upper part rising with abundance of handsome buildings;" and his continuator, Bishop Gibson, in the reign of Anne, mentions "its artificers in iron and steel, whose performances in that way are greatly admired both at home and abroad." Prior to the restoration of Charles II. the town only consisted of one long street, extending from the hamlet of Deritend to the present Bull-street, and contained barely 5,000 inhabitants. *Now*, the probably correct amount would stand thus: streets, 340; houses, 22,000; population, 200,000. Birmingham was created a borough by the Reform Bill, and sends two members to parliament. The honours of a mayor and corporation are now added to its civil dignities.

Among the almost innumerable branches of trade and manufacture at present carried on, are light and heavy steel goods, (here called toys,) brass and iron foundery, sadlery, military accoutrements, fire-arms, swords and cutlery of various kinds; jewellery, gold, silver, and plated goods; buttons, medals, japannery; gilt, silver, ivory, bone, and other toys; glass, wood-turnery, metal-rolling, tools and implements of all kinds; mill machinery of all sorts, and steam engines on every known principle. Casting, modelling, die-sinking, engraving, and other processes connected with the various manufactures have been brought to the greatest perfection; also the cutting of glass, of which there are many brilliant specimens in the show-rooms of the town, especially those of Messrs. Rollason, Price, Henderson, Mrs. Bedford's, &c. The great establishment at the Soho, near Birmingham, is intimately connected with its manufacturing interests, as under the superintendence of Messrs. Boulton and Watt, great improvements were effected in all kinds of machinery, and the power of steam applied to every mechanical purpose. From their ingenious coining mill, the greater part of the copper money of George III. was issued. Mr. Boulton died in 1809, aged eighty-one, and Mr. Watt in 1819, aged eighty-three. They were both interred in Handsworth church, where a marble bust commemorates the former, and a statue, by Chantrey, the latter.

In the magnificent show-rooms of Mr. G. R. Collis in Church-street, (formerly Sir E. Thomason's,) splendid specimens of the chief native manufactures are collected, and their mode of manufacture shown to all respectable visitors. Mr. Phipson's pin manufactory, which in this seemingly small article employs so great a number as one thousand persons, is another large establishment; and the articles of oriental gorgeousness and diversity, displayed by Messrs. Jennens and Betteridge, at their japanned ware and papier maché manufactory, in Constitution-hill, are full of brilliant designs and adornment. The show-rooms of Messrs. Mapplebeck and Lowe, Osborne, and others, contain a great variety of hardware and cutlery.

Of ponderous machinery, none perhaps is more interesting than that of the metal rolling mills; there is positive grandeur in the great power employed, and the accuracy with which it is adjusted to the end required. The button manufacture is a principal source of wealth to the town, and many of its chief families may trace back their origin (their *honourable* origin—far more truly honourable than the anxiety occasionally shown by present full-blown importance to disguise it) to a humble fabricator of these small and indispensable articles. They are made of all kinds and descriptions, to suit all markets; as were buckles likewise, some years since; but fashion, that mighty revolutionist, has driven them from their once prominent station in the toilet of the exquisite of former days; and knees and shoes, and dainty spangled and high heeled slippers, fit for feminine feet, have all laid by the buckles which used to glitter in cut steel and silver delicately worked, or set with brilliants; and of so comely dimensions, as well nigh to cover the pretty insteps of our grandmothers. As a source of great wealth to our native town, we must regret the abolition of ornamental buckles. Steel tools, and lighter, tasteful articles, form another great branch. The first steel-house, or factory, gave the name "Steelhouse-lane" to the street. Guns were first made in the reign of William III., and in times of war have constituted an important part of our trade. Silver, brass, and iron are all wrought to a great extent, in every known variety of manufacture. To enumerate *all* the productions of Birmingham were nearly an impossible task, had we space; as it is, we must rest here, and proceed to notice a few of the chief buildings and institutions which would attract the observation of a stranger.

W. Green Del.

BIRMINGHAM TOWN HALL.

The exterior of the Building is of Anglesea White Marble.

Extreme length 265 feet	*Length of Hall 140 feet*
—— breadth 104 ——	*Breadth —— 65 ——*
—— height 83 ——	*Height —— 65*

First, of the first class, ranks our noble and magnificent Town Hall, in Paradise-street, a Grecian temple of the Corinthian order, standing on a rustic basement, and built of marble from Anglesea. It is of recent erection; from the design, and under the direction of Mr. J. Hansom, of Hinckley, and contains a splendid hall, 140 feet long, by 65 feet wide, and 65 feet high, adapted for great public meetings, and for the performances of music at the Triennial Festivals; * it also contains spacious saloons, committee rooms, &c. Its organ is the finest in the kingdom. The new Free Grammar School, in New-street, is a large and handsome building, in the Gothic style, from a design by Mr. Barry, of London. The exhibition rooms of the Birmingham Society of Arts, New-street, form a handsome building, admirably adapted for the purpose; and the annual exhibition, of ancient and modern masters, is inferior to no provincial one. Another spacious suite of rooms was erected a few years since, by a dissentient party of the artists; but, having returned to the parent institution, their gallery has since been occupied by the highly interesting, valuable, and well-arranged Museum of Natural History, collected by Mr. Weaver, in the various branches of geology, ornithology, entomology, mineralogy, conchology, &c., &c. The Royal School of Medicine and Surgery, in Paradise-street, have now purchased this splendid collection, which, joined to the one they already possess, will form one of the finest Museums in the

* The proceeds of the Musical Festivals are for the benefit of the General Hospital, and not given to the Dispensary, as is stated in Mr. Lacy's Liverpool Guide-book.

provinces. It is liberally supported and patronised by the neighbouring nobility and county families. The General Hospital, Blue Coat School, Dispensary, and Asylums, are worthy of all praise for their essential utility as charities. The former is mainly supported by the proceeds of the Triennial Festivals; the others by liberal subscriptions, with which the inhabitants of Birmingham appear ever ready to increase the usefulness of charities having for their end the alleviation of misery, in whatever form it exists. The new Market Hall, extending from the Bull-ring to Worcester-street, is a spacious and commodious building, though the internal arrangement might be greatly improved, by a little more attention to order and neatness on the part of the various trades-people who have stalls there. The market having formerly been held in the open street, may, in some degree, account for this. Nearly opposite the hall stands a statue of Lord Nelson, by Westmacott, with a miniature man-of-war beside him, on a pedestal surrounded by an iron rail and lamps.

The Churches most remarkable for architectural beauty, are, St. Philip's, in the Doric style, with a graceful tower and cupola: Trinity Church, Bordesley, designed by Mr. F. Goodwin, much in the style of King's College Chapel, Cambridge; it is a fine example of the Ecclesiastical Gothic: St. George's, also Gothic, but of far inferior beauty: St. Martin's, which *has* been a fine old edifice, with a tapering spire, but is now disfigured by a brick shell: St. Paul's, Christ Church, St. Thomas's, St. Peter's, St. Bartholomew's, St. Mary's, All Saints', and others are of less striking appearance.

Many of the dissenting congregations have handsome and spacious meeting-houses and chapels, particularly the Catholic Chapels; Unitarian Meeting-houses; Independent Meeting-house, Carr's-lane; Mount Zion Chapel; Scottish Kirk, &c. Schools are connected with all, and with the numerous National, Lancasterian, Infant, and other schools, combine in distributing knowledge, in however a small degree as yet, among the useful and industrious classes. The excellent school for the instruction of Deaf and Dumb children is pleasantly situated at Edgbaston: there are also various Asylums for the young, the helpless, and the immoral (repentant, of course).

The Old Library, in Union-street, contains a valuable collection of 40,000 volumes, and commodious reading rooms. The New Library, in Temple-row, is a more recent and smaller establishment. Divers conglomerations of novels, called "Circulating Libraries," also exist for the benefit of the sentimental. The Philosophical Institution has a convenient Lecture-Theatre and Museum in Cannon-street, with a resident Curator. Subscribers have the privilege of introducing strangers to the lectures. The members of the Mechanics' Institution at present have lectures in the same building, until the erection of one suitable for them. Strangers are admitted to the Mechanics' lectures on payment of one shilling. The Botanical and Horticultural Society have extensive gardens and conservatories at Edgbaston, situated on rising ground, and commanding a beautiful and richly-wooded expanse of scenery. The exhibitions of plants, fruits,

&c., when a brilliant company generally assembles, are scenes of great gaiety.

The Conservatories and Greenhouses, are the erection of Mr. T. Clark, of Lionel-street, Birmingham, whose manufactory for Metallic Hothouses, &c., is very extensive.

A Cemetery has been recently laid out and planted on the north side of the town, at Key Hill, where a large excavation in a hill of gravel renders the spot striking and even picturesque: a neat Chapel is erected for the performance of the funeral service.

In 1813 an Act of Parliament was obtained for the erection of a Proof House for all fire-arms made in the town, which are subjected to a very severe test. The hall and other premises are in Banbury-street, and have quite a military and formidable appearance.

The News Room, on Bennett's-hill, and the different banking establishments, are handsome buildings, many of them of considerable architectural beauty. The Theatre is large, and inferior to few out of the metropolis, though the indifferent encouragement given to the drama in Birmingham, causes it to be comparatively but little used. It is capable of accommodating 2,500 persons, and contains to the front, a suite of Assembly Rooms, Billiard and Coffee Rooms, &c. There were formerly two smaller theatres, and an amphitheatre for equestrian performances, all three of which have been converted from their dissolute ways, and become pious and holy conventicles for divine worship. Temporary amphitheatres have frequently been erected since, and a permanant one is in progress. For more circumstantial particulars and descriptions of these and other edifices, we must refer our readers to the "Picture of Birmingham,"* or other more lengthy histories.

The environs of the town, especially Edgbaston and Harborne, contain many tasteful residences, erected by the wealthier merchants and tradesmen; whose pretty suburban villas have all gardens and pleasure grounds attached. In the neighbourhood of Birmingham are many fine old houses, or halls, as they are called, well deserving of a visit from the antiquary or artist; and the far famed glories of Warwick, Kenilworth, Shakespeare-sainted Stratford, Guy's Cliff, and other places of renown, are within a short drive.

In this brief survey of the past and present condition of Birmingham, it will be seen how rapidly its greatness and importance have been achieved by the perseverance, spirit, and ingenuity of its inhabitants. We may expect as rapid, and almost as great improvements from the additional consequence and advantages it will receive from the great works now nearly completed. The finished line of railway from London to Liverpool through this place, may, with confidence, be looked to as another great era in its history, from whence to date still increasing wealth, power, and intelligence.

* "The Picture of Birmingham," published by J. Drake, New-street, containing an historical and descriptive account of the town, with an accurate map, and twelve views of the principal buildings, &c.

CHAPTER II.

ROUTE.

BIRMINGHAM TO WOLVERHAMPTON,

Fourteen Miles.

BIRMINGHAM AND VAUXHALL STATION.

Distance to Liverpool and Manchester, 97¼ miles.

DISTANCES BY ROADS FROM THIS STATION TO THE FOLLOWING PLACES:—

*** Those printed in small capitals are market towns.

Places W. of Station.		*Places E. of Station.*	
Edgbaston	2½ miles.	Erdington	3 miles.
Harborne	4 —	Castle Bromwich	4½ —
HALESOWEN	8½ —	SUTTON COLDFIELD ..	6½ —
STOURBRIDGE	12½ —	Water Orton	6½ —
		Curdworth	7½ —
		COLESHILL	8½ —
		Wishaw	9 —
		Middleton	9½ —
		Drayton Bassett	11½ —
		TAMWORTH	13 —

THE Birmingham Station of the Grand Junction railway, closely adjoins that of the London and Birmingham, which greatly facilitates the arrangements of travellers proceeding along the entire line. Until the completion of the permanent buildings, those at Vauxhall have been temporarily used. To a stranger coming into the station-yard for the first time, the whole scene is one of great novelty: the long train of treble-bodied coaches, waiting under a broad covered way for passengers and baggage; the bustle and animation of the host of porters, guards, conductors, &c.; the amazement depicted on some of the faces of the lookers-on; the state of "intellectual complication" evinced by others, especially those who, having various items of property to convey with them, are tremblingly solicitous for the welfare of sundry "red-striped carpet bags, trunks with wrappering over," bandboxes which will be ruined by a drop of rain, and fish-baskets which have a mortal antipathy to be squeezed. Other important-looking passengers make up their minds to take things as a matter of course, and not betray any vulgar surprise; and from their extremely over-done *nonchalance*, would fain persuade you they had made a journey round the globe in a first-rate train, and reached the antipodes by a tunnel. These valiant and adventurous individuals are by far the severest sufferers by the anti-cigar-act, passed by the Company, for which the unsmoking part of the community, especially the fair sex, are greatly indebted. The traveller may refer to the company's regulations at full, in the appendix at the end of this volume. Supposing all preliminaries adjusted, we commence our journey.

Passing the station at Vauxhall, (closely adjoining to which are Vauxhall Gardens,) the railroad proceeds by Duddeston, and passes over the Coleshill road near Saltley Chapel, a small pigeonhouse like edifice to the E. of the line. Aston Church soon appears on the W., above the rich woods surrounding it; and the high chimney of the Birmingham Water Works (lately established to supply the town) is passed on the E. The steam engines, Hercules and Atlas, erected here for pumping the water from the reservoir, into the pipes for conveyance to Birmingham, are perhaps the grandest and most perfect of their kind ever fabricated. Yardley Village and Perry Barr form the distant view. The railroad now passes over the Aston embankment, and a viaduct of ten arches, beneath which runs the high road to Sutton, and the Fazeley Canal. From this point the last view is gained of the town of Birmingham, on the W.; and on the E. a prospect of Gravelly Hill, now nearly levelled, and the village of Erdington. A short distance onwards the line passes the front of Aston Hall, a fine old baronial residence in the Elizabethan style of architecture, erected by Sir Thomas Holt in 1620, and in which he entertained Charles I. previously to the battle of Edge Hill. It is situated in a fine park, richly ornamented with stately timber of ancient growth, and thriving modern plantations. All the views of this fine old mansion are strikingly beautiful; but the one commanded from the railroad line, looking up the avenue of lofty elms, (which the line crosses,) is the most imposing.

James Watt, Esq., the present proprietor, has, it is said, expended £10,000 in preventing the line of railroad from passing through his park, which the Company intended it to do; and in consequence of this opposition a great curve appears in the course of the line at this part. Iron works in the neighbourhood have been in operation from remote antiquity.*

The Church, which re-appears at several points of the line, is a beautiful and venerable structure, with a fine tapering spire, and remarkably musical bells, the

* See page 2.

Harris, del. Edd. Roberts, sc.

Aston Hall.

sweet tones of which will scarcely reach the ears of railroad travellers. Part of the village of Aston is observable from the railroad, and also the grounds and fish-pans of its "Tavern," a spot much frequented by tea (and ale) drinking parties from Birmingham.

One very agreeable feature of the scenery on the line, is the unspoiled freshness and verdure of the ground on either side. The idea most persons entertain respecting such astounding innovations on ancient usages as steam carriages and railroads is, that they spread desolation around their path, and that the track of a locomotive engine must necessarily be as devastating in its effects as that of a lava course. We candidly confess to something akin to this suspicion ourselves. But all "Grand Junction" patrons must be gratified to find such expectations disappointed so pleasingly in the cheerful aspect of the fields, groves, and "little running brooks," closely bordering the excavations or embankments. Cattle are quietly feeding just on the other side the fence, and gay wild-flowers already enamel the newly-made banks. Sometimes, certainly, a horse or cow may be abruptly interrupted in a quiet meditation by the rapid rushing by of a "Centaur" or "Alecto," with its lengthened *tail* of many ponderous joints; and one accident, very singular, if true, occurred lately. A certain luckless individual of the pig family, having too far indulged an imprudent spirit of investigation on the Bilston portion of the line, had his curly conclusion very summarily amputated by a passing train:—he turned round briskly to ascertain the extent of his calamity, when another train, whirling along in an opposite direction, coming in contact with his head, put a period to the enterprising animal's existence by an instant decapitation. We might draw a wise and serious moral from this "cutting" event, but the fact presents a sufficient warning to all persons inclined to incur the penalty of two pounds in sterling coin, and limbs *ad libitum*, for the sake of a promenade on the forbidden ground. "Digression is a sin,"—on the defunct pig's head be ours! But for his tragic history, we should, ere this, have introduced the hill of these parts, Barr Beacon, to our readers; it appears to the N.E., crowned with a dense grove of trees. The intervening scenery is cheerful and cultivated, but not picturesque. The village of Witton shortly appears to the E., with Barr lying on the N.E. The bridge here passed is on the boundary of Warwickshire and Staffordshire, which latter county the line now enters. Aston Hall and Church again come in sight beyond Witton, and form a beautiful rear view, which is soon shut out by the banks of the excavation, precluding all prospect save of their own sloping sides, the pebbles and markings in which are made, by the rapidity of passing, to appear like flying lines.

Perry Barr Station.

Distance to Birmingham, 3½—Liverpool and Manchester, 94 miles.

DISTANCES BY ROADS FROM THIS STATION TO THE FOLLOWING PLACES:—

Places W. of Station.		*Places E. of Station.*	
Handsworth	1 mile.	Perry	¾ mile.
Aston	1 —	Erdington	2¾ miles.
Smethwick	4¼ miles.	SUTTON COLDFIELD ..	5 —
		Little Aston	6 —
		Shenstone	8½ —

Aston Church and Viaduct.

Published by J. Drake, Birmingham.

At this station, the line makes a considerable curve in an opposite direction to that hitherto followed, and passes Handsworth, (the church appearing among wood on the W.,) also Lea Hall, on the W., and over two bridges, named from J. Gough, Esq., through whose estate the line runs for two miles. Pleasant, quiet-looking scenery skirts the road for some distance, and about a mile from the last bridge, a view is gained of Perry Hall, seat of J. Gough, Esq., nearly encompassed by a grove of oak trees. At Hampstead Bridge, the old Walsall road crosses the line; and on either side the prospect is pleasantly varied by wood and water. Hampstead Hall, which lies near, is nearly concealed by its rich woods from the passers on the railroad. The line shortly enters a cutting, of from sixty to seventy feet deep; emerging from which into the open country, West Bromwich, and Sandwell Park, the seat of Earl Dartmouth, appear on the W., and Barr on the E. We now pass

Newton Road Station.

Distance to Birmingham, 6¾—Liverpool and Manchester, 90¾ miles.

DISTANCES BY ROADS FROM THIS STATION TO THE FOLLOWING PLACES :—

Places W. of Station.			*Place E. of Station.*		
West Bromwich	2	miles.	Great Barr	2½	miles.
Oldbury	3¼	—			
Rowley Regis	5	—			
Halesowen	7¼	—			
Cradley	7¼	—			
The Lye	8½	—			

West Bromwich has rapidly risen to importance from the rich iron and coal mines which abound in its vicinity. The great Gas Works are situated here, which supply the chief part of Birmingham, Wednesbury, Dudley, Bilston, Darlaston, and other places with gas; the main tubes extending to the aggregate length of 150 miles. There are two handsome churches, the one ancient, the other modern. Population, 15,330.

The site of the present splendid mansion of Sandwell, was, in the reign of Henry II., occupied by a priory of Benedictine Monks. Charley Mount, pleasantly situated on a hill, appears W. of the line, Ray Hall and Burslem, or Bustleholm Mill, on the E. Before passing Tame Bridge, Barr Beacon again appears, heading the distant view. Friar Park is on the W., with the town and church of Wednesbury (usually pronounced Wedgebury), towering above the trees. Walsall appears from the same point, lying N.E. of the line.

Dudley, a town in the centre of the mining district, lies 5½ miles W. of the line. Population, 23,050. The ancient castle is a ruin of great beauty and interest, situated on an eminence, and surrounded with fine wood and beautiful walks. Stupendous cavern-quarries, canals, and labyrinthine excavations, extend under the Castle Hill. The limestone is remarkably rich in fossil treasures; trilobites, or, as they are vulgarly called, "Dudley locusts," have been found here in great variety, but from the eagerness of collectors, and the inadequate supply of these ancient creatures yielded by the rocks, they have become scarce and costly, instead of "not particularly valuable," as stated by a contemporary before alluded to.

WEDNESBURY is a town of ancient origin, having been fortified against the Danes by Ethelfleda, daughter of Alfred the Great, in 916. Extensive collieries enrich the vicinity, and tend greatly to darken the complexion of both houses and inhabitants; the workers of the black diamond hereabout being a marvellously murky fraternity. Various manufactures of iron are here carried on, and the air is generally redolent of the fumes of coal-smoke in no small degree. The market is on Friday, and fairs May 6, and August 3.

WALSALL boasts an equally ancient history with the former place, and was fortified by the same princess. It stands conspicuously on the summit and acclivities of a limestone rock, which is crowned by the church, the lofty spire of which forms a fine object. Market on Tuesday; fairs September 24, Whit Monday, and Tuesday before Michaelmas day. Proceeding onwards we pass under

Bescot Bridge Station.

Distance to Birmingham, 9½—Liverpool and Manchester, 88 miles.

DISTANCES BY ROADS FROM THIS STATION TO THE FOLLOWING PLACES:—

Places W. of Station.		*Places E. of Station.*	
WEDNESBURY	1 mile.	WALSALL	1½ mile.
Tipton	4 miles.	Rushall	2½ miles.
DUDLEY	5½ —	Over Stonnal	6½ —
Netherton	6¾ —	Lower Stonnal	7½ —
Brierley Hill	8¼ —	Shenstone	9 —
King Swinford	8½ —	LICHFIELD	11 —
Wordesley	9¼ —		
The Lye	9¼ —		
STOURBRIDGE	9¾ —		
Old Swinford	10½ —		

THE main road from Wednesbury to Walsall crosses this bridge; pass Bescot Hall, (Mr. Marshall's,) on the E., and reach

James's Bridge Station.

Distance to Birmingham, $10\frac{1}{4}$—Liverpool and Manchester, $87\frac{1}{4}$ miles.

DISTANCES BY ROADS FROM THIS STATION TO THE FOLLOWING PLACES:—

Places W. of Station.		*Place E. of Station.*	
Darlaston	$\frac{3}{4}$ mile.	Walsall	$1\frac{3}{4}$ mile.
Coseley	3 miles.		

THE high road from Walsall crosses here to DARLASTON, (seen in the distance on the W.,) another town in the iron and coal district, and, according to tradition, the seat of Wulphere, king of Mercia, who put his two sons to death for embracing Christianity. On the hill at Berry Bank, are the remains of a large castle and entrenchments, and near by, a Barrow, which it were heresy to doubt were the residence and grave of this redoubtable personage. The chief manufactures of this, as of the neighbouring towns, consist of various iron and steel goods. The whole district is abundantly traversed by canals, tram-roads, &c., for the convenient conveyance of merchandise, and presents to the passing traveller less subject for praise in point of beauty, than for admiration and surprise, at the closely-placed engines, mills, coal-pits, iron-mines, and factories, which greet him on all sides, with hissing, curling volumes of white steam, or thick massy clouds of rolling smoke. Should the traveller journey through this strange neighbourhood by night, the novel and wild, not to say, grand, effect of the fires, must strike him forcibly. Huge furnaces glowing on the earth, from a dark way-side forge; tall chimneys, themselves not seen in the gloom, vomiting forth flames and fiery-coloured smoke, or a long range of glowing hillocks, where flickering blazes play from the charcoal burning within: add to these, the dusky figures of the men and boys employed in the works, and a stranger will have a scene before him, in which the "fearsome" is oddly enough blended with the grotesque.

In the distance, S.W. of the line, appear the Rowley Hills, a ridge of trap or basaltic rock, which, at the time of its elevation, upheaved and broke through the coal strata. The stone being hard and compact, the hills are quarried for paving flags, &c.

"The principal mass of these (trap rocks) occurs in the southern part of the county, overlying the coal-field which surrounds the town of Dudley. It there constitutes the material of a group of hills, beginning on the S. of that town, and terminating about half-way between Halesowen and Oldbury, a little beyond the village of Rowley. These hills consist of very pure basalt, which in the neighbourhood of Birmingham is called *Rowley rag*, because the village of Rowley is situated on one of these basalt hills; and this hill appears to the eye to be the highest of the whole range. These hills are all covered with soil; but quarries have been opened in many of them, and the basalt of which they are composed is employed for mending the roads. The streets of Birmingham are likewise paved with it. The columnar structure, though very frequent, is far from universal in this trap, which very commonly occurs in large spherical masses, decomposing on the surface into concentric layers. An amygdaloidal variety containing calcareous spar and zeolite occurs S. of Dudley. The highest point of the Rowley Hills is stated by Dr. Thompson to be 900 feet above the Thames at Brentford."—CONYBEARE AND PHILLIPS's *Geology of England and Wales.*

Passing through a cutting of considerable depth, we arrive at

Willenhall Station.

Distance to Birmingham, 12—Liverpool and Manchester, 85½ miles.

DISTANCES BY ROADS FROM THIS STATION TO THE FOLLOWING PLACES:—

Places W. of Station.			*Places E. of Station.*		
Bilston	1½	mile.	Bloxwich	3	miles.
Sedgley	4¼	miles.	Pelsall	4¾	—
Lower Gornal	5¾	—			
Himley	7¼	—			

The small town of Willenhall, at the period of the Norman survey, was called *Winehala*, the Saxon term for victory, probably from the great battle fought near it in 311. The village began to flourish in the reign of Elizabeth, when the iron manufacture was first established here: at present, it is noted for its collieries and flourishing trade in locks, and other articles of hardware. Population, about 5,900.

Nothing of particular interest occurs on either side of the line, till, in approaching the long Wednesfield tunnel, the geological traveller will observe the re-

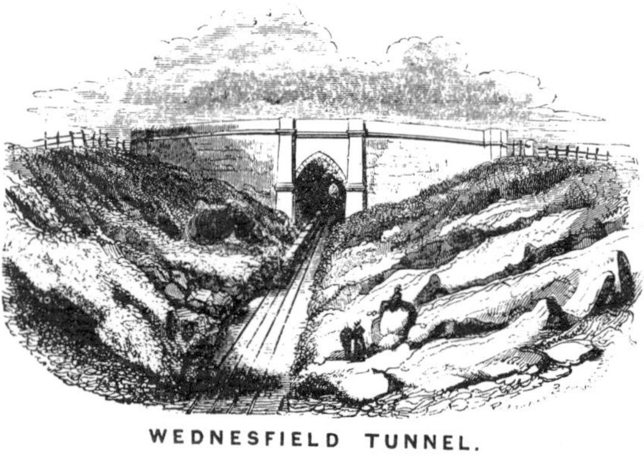

WEDNESFIELD TUNNEL.

markable section formed by the excavation through the outcropping beds of coal, which in this part rise at a great angle towards the surface, and are worked in the neighbourhood by open cuttings. The complete change which this abrupt ending of the coal-field causes in the aspect of the country is very singular. On one side all is black and murky; on the other, green and bright.

The tunnel is 180 yards in length, and the effect of a long train of carriages passing rapidly under, is novel and grand, nor less so the appearance of their emerging from the dark archway, to the expectant spectators at the

WOLVERHAMPTON STATION.

Distance to Birmingham, 14¼—Liverpool and Manchester, 83¼ miles.

DISTANCES BY ROADS FROM THIS STATION TO THE FOLLOWING PLACES:—

Places W. of Station.		*Places E. of Station.*	
WOLVERHAMPTON (Town)	1 mile.	Bushbury	1¾ mile.
Tettenhall	2 miles.	Wednesfield	1¾ —
Upper Penn	3½ —		
Codsall	4½ —		
Wombourne	5¼ —		
Himley	6 —		
Trysull	6 —		
Pattingham	6½ —		
Albrighton	7 —		
Donington	7½ —		
King Swinford	7½ —		
Bonningale	8 —		
BRIDGENORTH	14 —		
SHIFFNAL	14 —		

THE panting and smoking engine, like a huge beast, rushing along with fiery jaws, and "such a length of tail behind," might, in a dark night, be easily suspected of being "no canny." Divers kinds of vehicles, from post-chaises and landaus, to caravans and *omnibii* (as a refined friend of ours pluralizes these universal conveyances) are in attendance at this station, to convey passengers to the town of Wolverhampton, one mile distant, or to their future destination.

WOLVERHAMPTON is a place of considerable antiquity, and was called Hanton or Hampton prior to the year 996, when Wulfrana, sister of King Edgar, and widow of Aldhelm, Duke of Northampton, founded a college here, endowing it with so many privileges that the town was called in her honour, *Wulfranis Hampton*, of which its present name is evidently a corruption. The College continued till the year 1200, when Petrus Blesensis, who was then dean, after fruitless attempts to reform the dissolute lives of the brethren, surrendered the establishment to Hubert, archbishop of Canterbury, and it was subsequently annexed to the deanery of Windsor. In 1590, the greater part of the town was destroyed by a fire, which continued burning for five days. In the parliamentary war, Wolverhampton aided the royalists, and Prince Rupert fixed his head-quarters here, while the king was encamped at Bushbury.

The town is situated on an eminence, on the N.W. side of the great midland coal-district, and the neighbourhood abounds with iron, coal, and limestone. The manufacture of locks, forms here as in the other towns in the vicinity, the staple trade, to which may be added, smith's and carpenter's tools, machinery of all kinds, furnishing ironmongery, &c. The modern streets are well-built and lighted, and contain many handsome and substantial houses. A public Subscription Library and News-room, occupy the lower part of a commodious building, in which, assemblies and concerts are likewise held. A Literary and Philosophical Society is established, but not yet supported in a manner at all proportioned to its merits; a circumstance not reflecting much honour on the professedly intelligent and "higher" classes of the inhabitants. The Mechanics' Institution is in a more flourishing condition, for obvious reasons, being patronized by the more knowledge-loving part of the community. The Theatre is opened occasionally; it is a small and unpretending structure. Races are annually held in August, in an extensive area near the town, and are well attended. In the centre of the market-place stands a cast-iron column, forty-five feet high, surmounted by a large gas lantern, which was intended by its sanguine projector to enlighten the whole town and suburbs, but, alas for the great designs of short-sighted humanity!—its sphere of usefulness is unfortunately restricted to the attic and chamber windows of the houses immediately contiguous.

The Collegiate Church is an ancient and exceedingly beautiful cruciform structure, in the early decorated style of architecture, with a handsome square embattled tower rising from the centre. It contains a curious and elaborately-carved stone pulpit, formed of one entire block, an ancient font, and several interesting monuments. In the church-yard is a column, twenty feet high, greatly enriched with sculpture of various designs, supposed to be of either Saxon or Danish origin. There are several other churches in Wolverhampton, and many religious establishments belonging to various sects of dissenters; also a Free Grammar School, Blue Coat Charity, National, Sunday, and other Schools. The population of Wolverhampton is about 25,000; it has a market on Wednesday, and a fair on July 10.

CHAPTER III.

WOLVERHAMPTON TO STAFFORD,

Fifteen Miles.

On quitting the station at Wolverhampton a good view is obtained of the town and fine old Church, with the hills of Rowley Regis in the distance. Tettenhall Wood and the Clee Hills soon add to the beauty of the southward view; and the line is skirted by fine trees and fresh verdant meadows, over which a peep of the distant landscape is gained at intervals. Show Hill, and Low Hill houses are pleasantly situated on the ridge of a hill to the E., and beyond them appears Bushbury Hill, a point of the same elevation, with its old village

BUSHBURY HILL AND CHURCH.

Church, built about 1460; this is perhaps the most pleasing part of the line we have yet traversed. The Wrekin appears in the distance to the W., and nearer, the lofty and tapering spire of Brewood (or Brood) Church, rises from its girdling woods. Moseley Court, the ancient seat of J. G. Whitgreave, Esq., lies E. of the line, whence but little of the house is visible, being surrounded by stately oak groves. In this venerable mansion, Charles II. was temporarily concealed, when on his way to Bentley. Wrottesley Park, seat of Sir John Wrottesley, Bart., Chillington Park and Hall, the noble residence of T. W. Giffard, Esq., and the village of Codsall, form portions of the scenery to the S.W. All this part of the line from Wolverhampton is on an embankment, which, however, does not exceed fifteen feet at the highest point. On the E. appears Hilton Park, seat of H. E. C. V. Graham, Esq., and on the W., Pendeford Hall. The villages of Shareshill and Featherstone, lie E. of the line. A bridge here crosses it, bearing the felicitous name of "Paradise;" happy mortals, to reach such blessed bourne! But our stay is brief indeed; Paradise is left far behind, and we pass onwards under and over many a bridge of great and small degree; for the railroad even renders a common dirty gutter, a thing of so great importance, that a stately and ponderous arch must be erected for its insignificant accommodation! Verily, we grow aristocratic in our indignation at such upstart doings. The honourable fraternity of Ditch, Gutter, and Co., may, with a good grace, quote the old fable, and exclaim, "How we apples swim;" they are marvellously promoted since "an hundred years ago."

The Stafford Canal passes under, and the railroad over, a handsome iron bridge, between the village of Coven on the W., and Aspley on the E. side of the line.

The wide moorland called Cannock Chase, lies E., and is for some distance seen from the line. It was in earlier times, a forest or chase belonging to the Mercian kings. In one part, Castle Hill, now enclosed by the boundary of Beaudesert Park, seat of the Marquis of Anglesea, is an ancient British encampment, surrounded by a double trench, occupying about fourteen acres. Near it are the remains of a moat, enclosing an oblong square of three acres, called the Old Nunnery, where a Cistercian Abbey was founded in the reign of Stephen, which was shortly after removed to Stoneleigh, in Warwickshire. Cannock Chase, or Heath, contains upwards of 25,000 acres; in some parts, containing extensive sheep walks.

Four Ashes Station.

Distance to Birminghan, 20—Liverpool and Manchester, 77½ miles.

DISTANCES BY ROADS FROM THIS STATION TO THE FOLLOWING PLACES:—

Place W. of Station.		*Place E. of Station.*	
Brewood	2 miles.	Shareshill	2¾ miles.

If the reader be a passenger in a mixed train, the diminished speed will here allow him a better chance of observation; and a fine view may be enjoyed on the eastward, of Cannock Chase, with its undulating scenery; and westward, Summerford Park, seat of the Hon. E. Monkton, the little town of Brewood, and the Wrekin. Passing on, nothing of interest occurs until the arrival at the next, the

Spread Eagle Station.

Distance to Birmingham, 21½—Liverpool and Manchester, 76 miles.

DISTANCES BY ROADS FROM THIS STATION TO THE FOLLOWING PLACES:—

Places W. of Station.		*Places E. of Station.*	
Stretton	2 miles.	CANNOCK	4½ miles.
Lapley	3 —	Norton	6¼ —
Wheaton Aston	4¼ —		
Weston-under-Lizzard	7 —		
Blymhill	7 —		
Tong	8½ —		
Sheriff Hales	10½ —		
Woodcote	11 —		
SHIFFNAL	12 —		
WELLINGTON	17 —		
SHREWSBURY	29 —		

HERE the railroad crosses the old Roman road called Watling-street; the ancient prætorian highway, reaching from Dover, by St. Albans, Dunstable, Towcester, Atherstone, Shrewsbury, &c., to Cardigan; in many places it is scarcely perceptible, while in others it continues firm for several miles. And who can pass *such* a junction of roads, without a backward glance at past years and events? without a thought of the thousand "changes of time and tide" that this ancient track has witnessed: the millions of human footsteps it has received:—the proud and victorious Roman, exulting in his country's greatness and conquests, and contemptuously spurning the savage natives, whose natural rights he invaded:—the rapacious and desolating Dane:—the wily Saxon:—the adventurous Norman: and now the compound people, we English, who, not content with the ways of our fathers, must needs cross them with our refined and scientific innovations. In sooth, this ancient road were a fitter subject for an epic poem, than a guide-book gossip.

Passing the Spread Eagle station, the villages of Water Eaton and Stretton, are seen on the W., and Rodbaston Hall, with Cannock Chase behind, on the E. The turnpike road here runs parallel with the line for some distance. At Quarry Bridge, a short distance from Penkridge, is a fine quarry of red sandstone, which has furnished a handsome material for several bridges in the vicinity. From hence the church of Penkridge, and the next arch over the line, forms an interesting picture, to which the near arch of Quarry Bridge serves as framework.

PENKRIDGE CHURCH, FROM QUARRY BRIDGE.

The church is shortly after passed, on the E., and arriving at the bridge over the river Penk, a lovely view of the surrounding scenery presents itself. The river appears on both sides, winding gracefully along, between meadows and groves; on the E. is

J. Wallace, del. J. Greig, sc.

Penkridge.

Published by J. Drake, Birmingham.

the Old Bridge, beyond which appears Teddesley Park and Hall, the seat of Lord Hatherton, with our old friend Cannock Chase in the distance. Westward the eye ranges over the near objects to Preston Hill and Longridge, altogether forming a delightful prospect.

Penkridge Station.

Distance to Birmingham, 24—Liverpool and Manchester, 73½ miles.

DISTANCES BY ROADS FROM THIS STATION TO THE FOLLOWING PLACES:—

Places W. of Station.			*Places E. of Station.*		
Bradley	3¾	miles.	Dunstan	2½	miles.
Church Eaton	5¼	—	Acton Trussel	2¾	—
			Bednall	3½	—
			CANNOCK	5	—
			RUGELEY	8	—
			Armitage	10½	—
			Malvesyn Ridware	11	—
			Longdon	11½	—

PENKRIDGE is supposed by Camden to have been the Roman Pennocrucium; its modern name seems derivable from the river Penk, on which it stands.

The town, from its low situation, is liable to frequent inundations. It has no market-day, but two great cattle fairs are held here, on April 30, and first Monday in September. The Church was made collegiate by King John. Penkridge contains about 3,000 inhabitants. Quitting Penkridge, the villages of Thickerscote and Silkmoor appear in the distance; and shortly after leaving Acton Trussel to the E., and Levedale on the W., Dunstan Church, appears above the bank of the railway, on the E. The next object of interest is Stafford Castle, the tower of which is seen just before arriving at

STAFFORD STATION.

Distance to Birmingham, 29¼—Liverpool and Manchester, 68¼ miles.

DISTANCES BY ROADS FROM THIS STATION TO THE FOLLOWING PLACES:—

Places W. of Station.			*Places E. of Station*		
Castlechurch	1	mile.	Baswick or Berkswick	1½	mile.
Coppenhall	2½	miles.	Marston	3¼	miles.
Houghton	4	—	Tixall	4	—
Gnosnal	7	—	Ingestre	4	—
NEWPORT	12	—	Weston	4½	—
			Sandon	5	—
			Gayton	5½	—
			Stowe	6¾	—
			Colwich	6¾	—
			Milwich	7	—
			Fradswell	7½	—
			Hilderston	8	—
			RUGELEY	9	—
			Gratwich	11	—
			ABBOTS BROMLEY	11	—
			UTTOXETER	14	—
			LICHFIELD	17	—

STAFFORD is a borough and market town; contains 8,512 inhabitants. This place, which is of great antiquity, was anciently called *Studeford*, from the Saxon Stade, signifying a place on a river, and the *trajectus*, or ford, across the river Sow, on which it is pleasantly situated, about six miles from its confluence with the Trent.

The entrance from the London road, is by a neat bridge over the river, near which was one of the ancient gates. The houses are in general well-built, and many of them are handsome and modern erections; the streets well paved, and the environs of the town abound with elegant mansions and villas. Assemblies are held in a suite of rooms in the Town Hall, and races take place annually in May. The chief branch of manufacture is that of shoes, and the tanning of leather is carried on to a considerable extent. Stafford is also renowned for its ale, in common with the surrounding neighbourhood. The market is held on Saturday, and fairs on April 5, May 14, June 25, October 3, and December 5.

Stafford Castle

Published by J. Drake, Birmingham.

From the year 700, this place has been gradually acquiring importance, and castles have been built and rebuilt by successive princes and possessors. In 705, it is said to have been the residence of the pious St. Bertalin, son of a Mercian king, and we may well imagine a *royal* hermitage to have formed an attractive nucleus for a future city. Ethelfleda, Countess of Mercia, erected a castle here in 913, and fortified the town with walls and a fosse. It appears to have increased greatly in extent and importance, and is in Doomsday Book called a city, in which the king had eighteen burgesses in demesne, and the Earl of Mercia twenty mansions. William the Conqueror built a castle here, to keep the barons in subjection, and appointed as governor, Robert de Tœni, the progenitor of the house of Stafford. It was rebuilt in the reign of Edward III., and in the parliamentary war was garrisoned for the king, but taken by the parliamentary troops, and finally demolished. The lover of picturesque relics of the olden time, must regret the utter destruction of this, and many other strong holds; but the knowledge, that the iron-handed tyranny upheld by these feudal dens, is for ever gone by with their departed strength, is a glorious and surpassing compensation. Where would be our railroads, if moss-trooping barons and slavish serfs formed, as they once did, the population of England?

The castellated building which now forms so prominent a feature in the landscape on approaching Stafford, is a modern erection, on the ancient site, commenced by Lord Stafford, (then Sir George Jerningham); only one front, flanked by two round towers was completed; these now contain some ancient armour and other curiosities. The County Hall is a spacious and handsome building of stone, occupying one side of the Market-place. The County Gaol is also a large and modern erection, well adapted for the classification of prisoners, who are employed at their trades, and receive a certain portion of their earnings on discharge.

The Church, dedicated to St. Mary, formerly collegiate, is an ancient and spacious cruciform structure, in the early style of English architecture, with a lofty octagonal tower rising from the intersection. The north entrance is richly ornamented, and the interior beautifully arranged, the piers and arches are of the early English, passing into the decorated style. The east window is an elegant specimen of the later English. In the north transept is an ancient font of great beauty, highly ornamented with sculptured figures and animals. There are many ancient monuments; amongst the most conspicuous, are those of the family of Aston, of Tixall. There are two other Churches, one, St. Chadd's, originally in the Norman style, but much and incongruously altered; also, places of worship for the Society of Friends, Independents, Wesleyan Methodists, and Roman Catholics. The Free Grammar School was refounded by Edward VI.; there are also National and other Schools, and a variety of Public Institutions, among which the Infirmary, and Lunatic Asylum are the chief.

In olden times, a Priory of Black Canons existed

here, founded in 1151; a small part of whose ruined abode remains, in the shape of a farm house, two miles east of the town. There were likewise, a House of Friars Eremites; a Priory of Franciscan Friars, and other monastic establishments, all dismantled at the dissolution. The most celebrated native of Stafford, is Isaac Walton, the angler, a name well-beloved by all votaries of the (so called) "*gentle* sport," though there are and have been many who rather think with the Poet, that

> "The quaint, old, cruel coxcomb, in his gullet
> Should have a hook, and a small trout to pull it."
>
> BYRON.

CHAPTER IV.

STAFFORD TO WHITMORE,

Fourteen Miles.

In leaving Stafford station, the Castle appears to the W. and the Town, E. of the line. Beacon Hill is seen immediately over the latter. On proceeding a short distance through a flat country, the little village of Aston is passed on the W., and Creswell Hall, (Rev. T. Whitley,) on the E., which, encompassed by richly wooded grounds, and overlooking the meanderings of the little river Sow, forms a fine object in the general landscape. The house is a plain, neat structure. Much of the ground here is marshy, and abounds with willows, whose light silvery foliage agreeably diversifies the meadow and woodland scenery; amid which, on the W., peeps the pretty tower of Seighford Church.

Passing two successive cuttings of no great depth, and through a marshy district adorned by poplar and willow trees, we arrive at

Bridgeford Station.

Distance to Birmingham, 32¾—Liverpool and Manchester, 64¾ miles.

DISTANCES BY ROADS FROM THIS STATION TO THE FOLLOWING PLACES:—

Places W. of Station.		
Seighford	1	mile.
Ranton	2¾	miles.
Ellenhall	3	—
Norbury	7½	—

On the E. is Bridgeford Hall, the estate of J. Reynolds, Esq., formerly a Convent. Some remains of the ancient buildings still exist in different parts of the hall and garden.

A story of a subterranean passage also belongs to this relic of olden times, which passage, says tradition, leads to Ellenhall, about two miles distant; and we have been told that in digging a well a few years since the passage was discovered.

A picturesque Mill stands near the Hall. Passing Chebsey W., and Whitgreave on the E., we reach Shallowford, where a few scattered cottages represent the honours of the Village, and the Sow, which almost emulates the winding propensities of the fair river Wye, meanders quietly among the meadows. At Shallowford Bridge, which is chiefly built for the convenience of farmers, whose cattle and teams are constantly traversing it, a person is generally stationed with a red flag to give a signal for trains to slacken their speed at this part, if cattle are passing at the time.

A pleasant but not very interesting portion of the line brings us to

Norton Bridge Station.

Distance to Birmingham, 35—Liverpool and Manchester, 62½ miles.

DISTANCES BY ROADS FROM THIS STATION TO THE FOLLOWING PLACES:—

Places W. of Station.			*Places E. of Station.*		
Chebsey	1¼	mile.	STONE	3	miles.
ECCLESHALL	2½	miles.	Swinnerton	4½	—
Standon	5	—	Hilderston	6¼	—
High Oftley	6½	—	Barlaston	6½	—
Adbaston	6½	—	Fulford	7½	—
Cheswardine	9½	—	Trentham	8	—
Hinstock	13	—	Draycott	9½	—
			LANE END	10	—
			CHEADLE	14	—

Two miles and a half W. of this station lies the small town of Eccleshall, which at the time of the Conquest belonged to the See of Lichfield. In 1200, Bishop Muschamp obtained a licence from King John, to embattle the episcopal residence; which was much repaired, or rebuilt, by Bishop Langton in 1310. During the parliamentary war it was so much damaged in a siege, previously to being taken by the parliamentarians, as to be unfit for the further residence of the church-militant commanders-in-chief, until Bishop Lloyd rebuilt it in 1695; since which time it has continued to be the episcopal palace of the See of Lichfield and Coventry. The grounds and woods belonging to the palace are pleasant and extensive. The church was the sanctuary of Queen Margaret, after Lord Audley's defeat by the Earl of Salisbury, at Blore Heath. It is a spacious structure, in the ancient English style of architecture, and contains several monuments.

The town of Stone lies three miles E. of the line, and is not seen from it; the name is traditionally derived from a monumental heap of stones, which, according to the custom of the Saxons had been placed over the bodies of the princess Wulford and Rufinus, who were here slain by their father king Wulphere, on account of their conversion to Christianity. [*See page* 20.] The king himself becoming subsequently a convert, founded, in 670, a college of Secular Canons, dedicating it to his children, in expiation of his crime: and to this establishment the town is supposed to owe its origin. The prevailing manufacture is that of shoes. Population, 7,808.

Although none of the towns in the great district called the Potteries, are upon or even seen from the line of route, yet they lie so near, that it would scarcely be well to omit all mention of this great manufacturing neighbourhood, which encloses about ten square miles of country, covered with scattered villages, and containing about 20,000 inhabitants. Although the making of articles of pottery has been carried on here from a remote period, yet the manufacture was of inferior importance, until the great improvements effected by Mr. Wedgewood in the latter part of the last century; since which time the excellence and beauty of the wares, have produced a most extensive traffic both in England and abroad. The exports of earthenware and china to the United States alone, amount to 60,000 packages annually. The several species of ware invented by Mr. Wedgewood, varied by the industry and ingenuity of the manufacturers into an infinity of forms, and differently painted and embellished, constitute nearly the whole of the fine earthenwares at present manufactured in England, which are the object of a very extensive trade. The chief towns and villages in the Pottery district are, Stoke-upon-Trent, Hanley, Burslem, Lane End, Shelton, Etruria, Tunstall, Lane Delph, and others.

Proceeding from Norton Bridge, through some pretty, common-place country, we pass Baddenhall, Field Cross, and Brockton-house on the W., and Coldmese on the E., and soon gain a view of Swinnerton Park and Hall, seat of T. Fitzherbert, Esq., which, with the small grove-like woods scattered through the landscape, forms, as the quaint Dugdale would say, "a verye faire prospect." The next small representation of a village is Mill Meese, with its old Hall standing close beside the line; the water-mill wheel, formerly accustomed to have no rival sound interrupt its rumbling, splashing solo, now seems wofully outdone by the rapidly rolling trains, and lifts up its unheard voice in vain. The river Sow still flows close to the line. Westward lie the villages of Walford and Aspley, but too much concealed by wood to be discovered in passing. Trentham Park, seat of the Marquis of Sutherland, is perceived on the N.E. The mansion is a modern structure; the surrounding grounds are very extensive, abound with fine timber, and greatly adorned by lakes, formed by the river Trent, which flows through the park.

Standon Church, with the richly wooded country round, forms a pleasing object W. of the line.

STANDON CHURCH.

Passing on, another Swinnerton Park appears on the E., there being two of that name. Hill Chorlton and Chapel Chorlton, with the picturesque church tower of the latter, appears W. of the traveller. A short distance of pretty wooded scenery intervenes, and then a shallow cutting, passing which, Maer Wood is seen on the W. Maer Hall, seat of J. Wedgewood, Esq.

Shortly after, the line enters a deep cutting, which ends at

WHITMORE STATION.

Distance to Birmingham, 43¼—Liverpool and Manchester, 54¼ miles.

DISTANCES BY ROADS FROM THIS STATION TO THE FOLLOWING PLACES:—

Places W. of Station.			*Places E. of Station.*		
Maer	1¾	mile.	NEWCASTLE-UNDER-LYME	5	miles.
Chapel Chorlton	3	miles.	Trentham	5	—
Ashley	3½	—	Wolstanton	6½	—
Standon	5	—	Shelton	7	—
Broughton	5½	—	STOKE	7	—
Mucklestone or Muxton	6	—	BURSLEM	7½	—
Norton	7½	—	HANLEY	7½	—
MARKET DRAYTON ..	10	—	Tunstall	8½	—
			LANE END	8½	—
			Norton-on-the-Moor	9	—
			LEEK	16	—

CHAPTER V.

WHITMORE TO CREWE,

Ten and ¾ Miles.

An extensive heathy bog is traversed by the line, after leaving Whitmore station, and, as we have heard an ancient tradition anent it, will tell the tale for the edification of our readers, " extenuating nothing."

Once upon a time there was a large forest in this part, and when the Romans were amusing themselves with hunting our worthy ancestors, a large body of the ancient Britons took refuge therein. In order to come at them these terrible Romans set fire to the forest, which burnt in a very fearful and dreadful manner; but our information does not extend to the exact measure of scorching endured by the miserable prisoners within this fiery fence, or whether they escaped by flight, or were consumed wholesale in the burning forest, which, with the accumulation of vegetable matter during past ages, has formed the bog, now "passed with the swiftness of tornado-blast," by "Wildfires" and "Rockets."

Opposite the Bog-house is one of the highest points of the line, the road inclining towards Liverpool one way, and towards Birmingham the other. Snape Hall is prettily situated among rich woods on the E. of the line; and a short distance farther Barr Hill appears on the W. It is a considerable elevation, and on a clear day, Liverpool may be seen from it. Madeley Parks and Manor House lie W. of the line. The latter is the seat of Lady Cunliffe, daughter of Lord Crewe, to whose family, the adjoining land, formerly a fine deer park, anciently belonged. Hay House, a small, old, brick building, stands close to the line of railway on the E. One cannot help feeling an odd sort of commiseration for these ancient abodes of the last generation, which have stood, and grown old and grey, in the once quiet and out-of-the-world nooks where the convenience of the farmer, or the retired taste of the small country squire, had located them; and now, to see the iron ribs of the innovating railroad carried up to their very threshold, has something of sadness in it, even in the midst of our modern pride and gratulation. It is like pert youth, exhibiting and vaunting of its strength and valorous deeds, to decrepid and helpless age. But what have we to do with such dreams? "Locomotives" wait for no man's fancies, and we must e'en follow their course. Soon after passing which, we reach

Madeley Station.

Distance to Birmingham, 46—Liverpool and Manchester, 51½ miles.

DISTANCES BY ROADS FROM THIS STATION TO THE FOLLOWING PLACES:—

Places W. of Station.			*Places E. of Station.*		
Woore	2¾	miles.	Betley	3	miles.
Norton	5½	—	NEWCASTLE	5	—
Mucklestone or Muxton	5½	—			
Audlem	7	—			
Adderley	9½	—			
Burley Dam	11	—			
WHITCHURCH	15	—			

THE village, which is rather eastward of the line, consists chiefly of cottages and farm houses in the Elizabethan style. The Church is an ancient and interesting structure, with a fine set of bells. An eccentric, named Samuel Stretch, noted for his penurious habits, bequeathed, in 1804, a great bell, to be tolled every night at eight o'clock, as a guide to persons wandering about at such late and improper hours; he having accidently fallen into a ditch, the consequences of which disaster eventually caused his death. The small town of Woore lies three miles W. Passing several slight cuttings, and again gaining the open country, a fine prospect appears, including Checkley Wood, Doddington Park, on the W., Heighley Castle on the E., and the Welsh Hills in the distance. Doddington Hall, seat of Lieut. Gen. Sir John Delves Broughton, Bart., is a splendid mansion of comparatively modern erection. A fortified house was erected here in 1364, by Sir John Delves, the venerable ruins of which still remain. The park is finely wooded, and includes a very noble avenue of ancient oaks. Heighley Castle partakes the traditionary honour so lavishly bestowed on such places, of having been "battered down" by Cromwell. It has been said, "no man can be in two places at once, unless he be a *bird.*" And our renowned Oliver must needs have been wonderfully endowed with this ornithological ubiquity, if we are to allow a shade of credence to the countless and unaccountable stories of his sieges *in propria personâ*. A lofty embankment and two viaducts carry the line through the pretty valley of Wrinehill; the Hall and Mill forming very pleasing objects in the scene. The line here enters Cheshire. Betley and Betley Mere form the next view, after emerging from a short excavation, called

Bunker's Hill. Betley Court, the residence of J. Twemlow, Esq., with its surrounding woods and fields, and the pretty mere or lakelet in front, afford a very pleasing view.

In the rear distance, S.E., is a fine view of Boond Hill and Mow Copp, on the round summit of the latter is a stone monument, distinctly seen. These hills, which lie at a considerable distance, join in the landscape for some space. Chorlton is the first village we pass in Cheshire, and Wybunbury, a place of much more importance, is concealed by the woods about the former, except the Church, which peers above them. This Church was rebuilt in 1595; it is a spacious structure, with carved wooden ceilings, and a lofty pinnacled tower, which leaned so much to the N.E., that a few years since it was found requisite to place it erect, when some alterations were made in the body of the Church. To the W. is Basford Hall, soon after passing which, we arrive at

Basford Station.

Distance to Birmingham, 52—Liverpool and Manchester, 45½ miles.

DISTANCES BY ROADS FROM THIS STATION TO THE FOLLOWING PLACES:—

Places W. of Station.			*Place E. of Station.*		
Hough	½	mile.	Betley	2	miles.
Wybunbury	1¼	—	Barthomley..	3	—
Walgherton	2	miles.	Audley	4	—
Doddington	2½	—	Alsager	5	—
NANTWICH	4	—	Talk	6	—
Audlem	5	—	Church Lawton	6	—
Burley Dam	7	—			
Baddiley	7	—			
Wrenbury	9	—			

CREWE HALL, the mansion of Lord Crewe, which

appears E. of the line, is a large and handsome quadrangular structure of red brick, surrounded by finely undulating grounds, and a lake of considerable extent.

CREWE STATION.

Distance to Birmingham, 54—Liverpool and Manchester, 43½ miles.

DISTANCES BY ROADS FROM THIS STATION TO THE FOLLOWING PLACES:—

Places W. of Station.		*Places E. of Station.*	
NANTWICH	4 miles.	Haslington	2 miles.
Acton	5¼ —	SANDBACH	5 —
Baddiley	7½ —	Astbury	10 —
Wrenbury	9 —	CONGLETON	11 —
MALPAS	17 —	Gawsworth	13½ —
		MACCLESFIELD	19 —

NANTWICH, four miles W. of Crewe, contains 5,350 inhabitants, and has a market on Saturdays, and fairs, chiefly for cattle, on March 26, second Tuesday in June, September 4, and December 4.

Previously to the Conquest, the wealth of this place consisted in its numerous brine springs. Its origin is attributed to the Britons; and its name appears to be derived from the British word *Nant*, a brook or marsh, and the Saxon *vic*, by corruption *wich*, a vill, or settlement. The latter term seems generally attached to the names of towns where salt is made. This town has had its full share of plague, pestilence, and war, in times past, and twice suffered greatly from fire, in the years 1438 and 1583. During the civil war it staunchly supported the parliament.

The town is situated on the banks of the river Weaver, in a level and fertile tract of country. Most of the houses are of timber and brick, covered with plaster, with projecting stories, and large bay-windows. There is a small Theatre and Assembly-room. In the time of Henry VIII., there were three hundred salt works; this number has been gradually reduced, in consequence of superior mines and springs being discovered elsewhere, and now only one spring remains. Shoes, gloves, and cotton goods are the chief manufactures now, and cheese the principal agricultural produce. The Church is a spacious and venerable structure, in the decorated and later English styles, comprising a nave, with lateral aisles, a chancel, transepts, and an ornamented octagonal tower, rising from the intersection. There are Meetings and Chapels for Dissenters, and various Schools. John Gerarde, whose fine old work, called Gerarde's Herbal, is familiar to every botanist, was a native of Nantwich, born in 1545.

CHAPTER VI.

CREWE TO HARTFORD,

Eleven and ¾ Miles.

QUITTING the Crewe station, around which is little to attract the traveller's notice, the line proceeds nearly without a curve, and for some distance enables the passengers of one train, to observe the approach of another. A branch railway is in progress from Crewe, to Manchester on one side, and to Chester on the other. The tower of Coppenhall Church is the first object on the W. This Church is an old wood and plaster structure, of the style prevalent in the reign of Elizabeth, and looking almost as if modern times had forgotten it, so quaint and old it is.

Passing the Church and Village, we arrive at

Coppenhall Station.

Distance to Birmingham, 56—Liverpool and Manchester, 41½ miles.

DISTANCES BY ROADS FROM THIS STATION TO THE FOLLOWING PLACES:—

Places W. of Station.		*Places E. of Station.*	
Minshull Moss	2 miles.	Coppenhall Moss	1 mile.
Lea Green	2 —	Warmingham	3 miles.
Leighton	2½ —	SANDBACH	5 —
Church Minshull	3½ —		
Worleston Green	4½ —		
Acton	5½ —		

The country near the line in this part becomes flat, boggy, and uninteresting; for though an ancient moss is a scene of uncloying interest to a naturalist, and contains many a treasure to reward the patient seeking of the botanist; yet, in the cursory glance of a railroad traveller, its sombre, and, as he perhaps thinks, unprofitable waste, is a scene gladly exchanged for verdant pastures and waving corn fields. Here is a whole family of mosses, all lying closely contiguous, and quaking under the foot of the pedestrian wanderer among their heathy labyrinths, "like a great jelly bag," as the graphic authoress of "Wood Leighton," that most graceful, good, and womanly book, quaintly describes a like spot. Coppenhall Moss, Leighton Moss, Warmington Moss, and, for aught we know, half a score more, compose the near view, with the welcome variety afforded by Warmingham Wood in the distance.

The towns of Sandbach and Congleton lie on the E., but are not seen from the line. The former contains about 7,200 inhabitants. The market is on Thursday, and fairs on Easter Tuesday and Wednesday, and the first Thursday after September 11; and a cattle and pleasure fair on December 27, for cattle and wearing apparel. In the market-place are some ancient crosses, repaired in 1816. The church is in the later English style. There are Dissenting Chapels, and several Schools. Congleton contains 9,352 individuals. It is an ancient place, and is called *Cogletone* in Doomsday Book, but its origin has not been clearly ascertained. The town is situated in a valley, embosomed in richly wooded hills: the eastern part is old and irregularly built; the western is modern. In the environs, especially on the banks of the river, are many elegant mansions and villas. The market is on Saturday; the fairs on the Thursday before Shrovetide, May 12, July 12, and December 22. The Market-house, containing a handsome Assembly-room, was built in 1822, at the sole expense of Sir E. Antrobus, Bart.

Minshull Vernon Station.

Distance to Birmingham, 58¾—Liverpool and Manchester, 38¾ miles.

DISTANCES BY ROADS FROM THIS STATION TO THE FOLLOWING PLACES:—

Places W. of Station.		*Places E. of Station.*	
Church Minshull	2 miles.	Warmingham	2½ miles.
Bunbury	6¾ —	SANDBACH	5 —
Tattenhall	12 —		
Harthill	12¼ —		

HERE the scenery becomes more interesting, from the distant view afforded on the W. of Beeston Castle Hill, and the high lands in Cheshire and Wales.

BEESTON HILL.

Beeston Castle was founded by Ranulph de Blundeville, about 1220, and was made a royal garrison, in the war between Henry III., and the confederate Barons. In 1643, Beeston Castle was held by a detachment of the Parliamentarian forces, then taken by the Royalists, who were, after a long siege in 1645, compelled, from want of provisions, to surrender it; and the Parliamentarians dismantled it early the following year. The ruins consist of part of a tower which guarded the principal entrance to the inner court, flanked by semi-circular bastions, and surrounded by a moat, excavated in the solid rock. The outer walls were defended by eight round towers, irregularly placed, and are now covered with ivy.

On the N.W. appears Delamere Forest, which continues to form part of the railroad prospect for some space. This tract, which includes the ancient and royal forest of Delamere, was uninclosed till 1812, when it was erected into a parish by act of parliament. It was formerly a dreary waste, but is now rapidly improving in fertility and increased population. On its enclosure, it first gave the title of Baron Delamere of Vale Royal, to Thomas Cholmondeley, Esq., the proprietor of the ancient possessions of the Cistercian monks of Vale Royal, whose sumptuous Abbey was completed in 1330, by Edward I., and cost £32,000. There are races in March, called the Tanfield Hunt.

Delamere Forest, comprising about 10,000 acres, once contained a great number of red and fallow deer: it exhibits a pleasing variety of well-wooded hills, rich valleys for pasturage, waters affording plenty of fish and water-fowl; and mosses, producing an abundance of peat and turf for fuel. Upon the highest hill stood the Saxon fortress of Finborrow, and near it the city of Eadesbury, both of which are said to have been founded by Ethelfleda, daughter of Alfred the Great. The ancient residence of the Chief Forester is all that now remains; this house is called the

Chamber of the Forest; and at convenient distances around it are neat lodges for the keepers of the several walks. Five thousand acres of the forest have been planted with forest trees within the last twenty years. The remaining portion is sold or allotted to private individuals.

Journeying on, we pass Lea Hall, a plain, old-fashioned building, close to the line, and can just perceive Over Church above the trees; this part of the line being more clothed with wood than that we have recently described. Here the Middlewich Canal is crossed, and is seen on the E., in which direction, two miles from the line, lies the town of Middlewich, containing about 4,800 inhabitants, with a market on Thursday, and fairs on Holy Thursday, Aug. 25, and Oct. 29. The name of this town is derived from its central situation with respect to the Wiches, or Salt Towns. A Roman station is supposed to have existed here, from the remains of a Roman road, and an intrenched camp. The Royalists were defeated here during the civil war, and the same fortune befel the Parliamentarian forces subsequently. The town is divided by the Grand Trunk Canal, here crossed by the river Dane; and the rivers Wever, Croco, and Whelock, also run through the parish. The chief trade consists in salt obtained from powerful brine-springs: there are also some silk manufactories. The church, being built at various periods, presents an assemblage of different styles of architecture: it has a handsome tower. Here are also dissenting meetings, and a free school, which, like many like establishments, fulfils, but in a very limited degree, the intentions of its founders. Delamere Forest and Over Church again form the westerly view.

The small straggling town of Over lies about a mile W. of the line; it contains 2,930 inhabitants; has no market, but fairs on May 15 and Sept. 25. The church was re-built in 1543, by Hugh Starkey, Gentleman Usher to Henry VIII., in the later English style of architecture. An effigy of brass in the interior of the church, perpetuates the memory of the pious Hugh; a curious font, and some other antiquities, may also be seen. Salt is the chief manufacture. In the extreme distance on the S.E., a clear day allows a tolerable view of the Derbyshire hills from this part of the line; Stanthorne Hall, seat of Richard Dutton, Esq., also E., is passed immediately before reaching the

Winsford Station.

Distance to Birmingham, 61¼—Liverpool and Manchester, 36¼ miles.

DISTANCES BY ROADS FROM THIS STATION TO THE FOLLOWING PLACES:—

Places W. of Station.		*Places E. of Station.*	
Over	2 miles.	MIDDLEWICH	2 miles.
Little Budworth	5¼ —	Brereton cum Smethwick	7½ —
TARPORLEY	8½ —	Swettenham	9½ —
Waverton	15 —	Nether Alderley	14½ —

BOSTOCK HALL, seat of James France France, Esq., and Wharton, *would* be seen E. from the railroad after leaving the station, but that the line enters a shallow cutting; the banks of which hide the view "just at the very time when they should not." An opening gives a glimpse of the woods about the house, and that is all. The next peep is westward again, at Moulson: and after passing another cutting (this word *cutting* is an inelegant term, which does not fall into our prose with ease; but we cannot avoid it, belonging, as it

E 3

does, to railroad phraseology) we gain a view of Vale Royal Park and New Park on the W., the pleasant woodland glades of which are soon shut out by another cutting which takes us through Eaton, and by Eaton Hall, seat of Sir E. Antrobus. We now approach one of the most magnificent parts of the railway, and of the scenery skirting it; the Vale Royal Viaduct, over which the line passes for five hundred feet, and beneath which the river Weaver winds through the vale in graceful sweeps, girt with verdant meadows; on the E. it is crossed by the simple old bridge, now looking very humble, in the presence of its magnificent neighbour. The viaduct consists of five arches of immense span, it is built of a reddish stone, and is a noble erection. The traveller will do well to be alert and on the "look out" in this part, or the view will escape him. Westward lies Vale Royal Park, rich in the grandeur of its ancient woods, and nearly hidden among them is Delamere Abbey, the old and venerable seat of Lord Delamere. Little remains now of the ancient building, which was not, as described by Warton in his Elegy, seen "high o'er the trackless heath," but was seated in a deep valley on the banks of the river Weaver. The present mansion consists of a centre and two wings of red stone. The great hall is a magnificent apartment.

The marvellous enlightenment of the 19th century, great as we deem it, has not yet penetrated those holes and corners of prejudice and credulity, which serve for the hiding places of superstition, for even in the eye of the Railroad itself are those living who speak with awe of the so-called prophecies, said to be made by the poor driveller Robert Nixon, the Cheshire sage. It so happens, very

Vale Royal Viaduct.

Published by J. Drake, Birmingham.

oddly, that predictions are sometimes remembered *when* verified, and not before. So was the curious and very oracular one of the past year, so often quoted,—

> " A summer without a spring,
> And an autumn without a king,"

which no one can deny was very remarkable indeed—only it was too disloyal to be circulated till certainty had secured its truth. Poor Nixon wishing, doubtlessly, to compliment his patrons, the Cholmondeley family, with a "May-the-king-live-for-ever" kind of benediction, promised that till certain stones or rocks near Warrington came to Vale Royal, the prosperity of their family should continue. Unluckily, stones have grown locomotive of late, and "Birnam Wood doth come to Dunsinane," for the fatal rocks have become part of the grand viaduct, which, far from bringing ill to the noble Delamere, is a link in the mighty chain now weaving, which shall bind together art, science, talent, wealth, and greatness, for the good of all who are so blessed as to live in the age of RAILROADS.

The line passes through a deep cutting before arriving at the

HARTFORD STATION.

Distance to Birmingham, 65¾—Liverpool and Manchester, 31¾ miles.

DISTANCES BY ROADS FROM THIS STATION TO THE FOLLOWING PLACES:—

Places W. of Station.			*Places E. of Station.*		
Newchurch	2¼	miles.	Davenham	1½	miles.
Little Budworth	5½	—	NORTHWICH	2	—
TARPORLEY	8	—	Great Budworth	6	—
Tarvin	10	—	NETHER KNUTSFORD ..	9	—
Great Barrow	11	—	Rostherne	10½	—
Guilden Sutton	13	—	Mobberley	11½	—
Waverton	13½	—	Wilmslow	15½	—
Christleton	13½	—			
CHESTER	16	—			

CHAPTER VII.

HARTFORD TO WARRINGTON,

Twelve and ¼ Miles.

PROCEEDING from the Hartford station, the banks of the cutting conceal much of the scenery. The small and scattered village of Gorstage appears on the W. From Hartford station to Acton station the evenness of the ground renders a train visible to a spectator, at either place, the entire distance.

The town of Northwich lies two miles E. of the railway; has a market on Friday, and fairs on April 10, for cattle only, August 2, and December 6. Camden is of opinion, that the brine springs here were used by the Romans, and says, the town was anciently called Hellah-Du, or the Black Salt Town. The town has a very antique appearance, and contains a church very remarkable for its semi-circular choir, and for the curious decorations of the roof of the nave, which consist of numerous figures of wicker baskets, similar to those used in the process of salt-making. The commercial prosperity of Northwich, is entirely dependent upon its numerous brine springs and extensive mines of rock salt; in which article the trade is so great, as to produce an annual export of 100,000 tons from the springs alone. They were discovered at a very early period, and are usually more than one hundred yards in depth. The brine, being raised by pumps set in motion by steam-engines, is conveyed by pipes into pans, thirty or forty feet square: these are fixed over furnaces, the heat arising from which, causes the water to evaporate, and the salt to crystallise; it is then drained and dried, and is fit for sale. The mines of rock salt were discovered in 1670, the upper stratum, lying about sixty yards below the surface of the earth, is ten yards thick. About 1772, a second stratum, ten feet thick, and of superior quality, was discovered, at the depth of one hundred and ten yards, the intermediate space being occupied by a solid mass of stone. This latter bed alone is worked by the following process:—A shaft is sunk, and on reaching the mine a roof of salt is left, supported by pillars of the same material. As the excavation proceeds, the fragments are raised in buckets by means of steam-engines. The pits form an area of two, three, or four acres, and when illuminated, present a singularly beautiful and magnificent appearance; the light being reflected from all points in every variety of hue, as from a promiscuous assemblage of mirrors and prisms. This fairy palace was the scene of an elegant entertainment, given by the spirited proprietors, to about a hundred of the members of the British Association, during the meeting at Liverpool, in 1837.

From an account published in 1818, it appeared that 200,000 tons of manufactured salt, and upwards of 40,000 tons of rock salt, were landed at Liverpool during the preceding year, and that upwards of 280,000 bushels are annually sold for internal consumption, by far the greatest proportion having been obtained in this neighbourhood; since that period the business has materially increased. The river Weaver and the Grand Trunk Canal afford great facilities for water-carriage from Northwich; and three hundred vessels are employed in the salt trade alone, which return laden with coal.

Passing through one or two slight cuttings, the line commands a fine view of Grange Hall, which stands on a well-wooded hill, near to the railway on the W. Eastward, is the village of Weaverham, and Winnington Hall, and, in the distance, the Overton Hills. The cutting at Acton Heath terminates near the

Acton Station.

Distance to Birmingham, 68¼—Liverpool and Manchester, 29¼ miles.

DISTANCES BY ROADS FROM THIS STATION TO THE FOLLOWING PLACES:—

Places W. of Station.		*Places E. of Station.*	
Crowton	1½ mile.	Weaverham..	1 mile.
Cuddington	1¾ —	Barnton	3 miles.
Kingsley	3 miles.	Great Budworth	5 —
Delamere House	3½ —		
Tarvin	10¼ —		

HAVING left Acton, the prospect is much impeded for some distance by the frequent cuttings through which the line passes; in the intervals, the Overton Hills appear on the W. Aston Hall (seat of the late H.C. Aston, Esq.) and grounds are shortly seen on the E., and immediately in front lies Dutton Wood. The traveller now approaches the magnificent viaduct crossing the river Weaver and the valley of Dutton.

This gigantic structure exceeds in magnitude anything of the kind yet accomplished in this country, or perhaps in Europe, not even excepting the Menai Bridge. The Viaduct is of the Gothic order, formed of red sand-stone procured from the neighbourhood of Bolton and Runcorn; it consists of twenty arches, of sixty feet span, and sixty feet in height, and the battlements add twelve feet more to the height; the whole length is 1,400 feet: 700,000 cubic feet of stone have been used in the work—the whole cost was £50,000.

The grandeur of this stupendous work is greatly enhanced by the richness and beauty of the adjacent country.

Completion of the Dutton Viaduct. On Friday, January 9, 1837, was performed the ceremony of laying the last, or key stone, of

Dutton Viaduct.

Published by J. Drake, Birmingham.

the magnificent viaduct across the Weaver, at Dutton. A party of the directors from Liverpool attended, and were met by Mr. Locke, the engineer, and the resident engineers and contractors on the line. Mr. Heyworth, as the senior director present, after placing the last stone in its bed, addressed the party. He congratulated the workmen (of whom about one hundred and fifty were present) on their steady perseverance and diligence in bringing to perfection so noble a work: he rejoiced to find, that, in the erection of this, the greatest and first structure of its kind in the kingdom, no life or limb had been sacrificed. Mr. Locke, the engineer, and the Rev. W. Stanhope, also addressed the meeting. The health of the workmen was then given by Mr. Locke, amid hearty cheers. In the evening, the viaduct was illuminated with torches, and fireworks were displayed in great abundance; during which time the workmen were regaled with a good dinner and excellent cheer.—*Chester Courant.*

The traveller who would enjoy glimpses of railroad views, must bear in mind the velocity of his conveyance, and prepare to "see whatever can be seen," or the most important objects will have glanced by the windows of his comfortable locomotive arm-chair coach, before any second person can warn him of their presence. Emerging from a cutting, which immediately succeeds the viaduct, Dutton Hall is observed on the E. backed by wood. A short distance farther, a fine rear-view is obtained (only by outside passengers we fear) of the Weaver, the vale of Dutton, Cogshall Park beyond, and in the distance the range of Derbyshire Hills. Passing between Bird Wood and Dutton Wood, we reach the tunnel at Preston Brook, 110 yards in length, over which the Chester road passes.

Preston Brook Station.

Distance to Birmingham, 72½—Liverpool and Manchester, 25 miles.

DISTANCES BY ROADS FROM THIS STATION TO THE FOLLOWING PLACES:—

Places W. of Station.	
FRODSHAM	3 miles.
Ince	9½ —
Plemondstall	10½ —
Thornton Le Moors	11½ —
Guilden Sutton	11½ —
Stoak or Stoke	12½ —
CHESTER	13 —
Backford	14 —

PRESTON, though a small place, is one of considerable traffic, from its vicinity to the salt districts, and to the Grand Trunk Canal.

Frodsham lies three miles W. of the line at this part; it has a market on Saturday, and fairs on May 15, and August 21. The principal branch of trade is salt refining, besides which, there are flour mills and cotton factories. This place is mentioned in Doomsday Book, as being the property of the Earl of Chester. The town, situated on an eminence on the banks of the Weaver, near its confluence with the Mersey, consists of a broad street, a mile in length; at the E. end is a bridge of four arches over the Weaver, and at the W. end anciently stood a Norman castle; another street leads to the Church, an ancient structure, partly in the Norman style of architecture.

Norton Priory, the residence of Sir Richard Brooke, Bart., is seen on the W. A religious establishment formerly existed here, some ancient parts of which are included in the present mansion. The Duke of Bridgewater's canal runs through the park. In the rear of Norton Priory, as seen from the railway, is the now busy and important town of Runcorn, containing 10,326 inhabitants.

In 915, Ethelfleda, sister to King Edward the Elder, widow of Ethelred, King of Mercia, built a town and castle near the river Mersey, at this place, some traces of which are still visible. In 1133, William Fitz Nigel founded here a monastery of canons regular, which, in the reign of Stephen, was removed to Norton Priory above mentioned.

Runcorn is a place of considerable resort for bathing, and has been recently much enlarged, and improved by handsome buildings, &c. The township abounds with fine stone quarries, from which great quantities are sent by water to Liverpool, Manchester, &c. Here are extensive chemical and soap works, in connexion with which a chimney of 273 feet in height, and of great beauty, has recently been erected. The church is in the early and later styles of English architecture. Near Runcorn are the fine ruins of Halton Castle, situated on a steep eminence, and commanding an extensive and beautifully varied prospect, including the Mersey estuary, the Welsh mountains, and richly-wooded scenery in Cheshire and Lancashire. This fortress was demolished during the civil wars. Eastward, passing Keakwick, and Daresbury, where is a fine old church, The Elms appear. Passing which we arrive at

Moore Station.

Distance to Birmingham, 75—Liverpool and Manchester, 22½ miles.

DISTANCES BY ROADS FROM THIS STATION TO THE FOLLOWING PLACES:—

Places W. of Station.		*Places E. of Station.*	
Halton	3½ miles.	Daresbury	1¼ mile.
Lower Runcorn	4 —	Hatton	2¼ miles.
Higher Runcorn	4½ —	Stretton	3¾ —
Weston	5 —	Grappenhall	4½ —

The pretty village of Moore is not seen from the line. Richly-wooded country lies on either side the road now, and occasionally peeping through the trees, the masts of vessels passing on the Mersey may be observed. The Mersey Viaduct is next traversed. This, though far less grand in appearance than the Dutton Viaduct, is a fine erection of 200 yards in length, consisting of twelve arches, nine being small, and three of larger span, beneath which the river Mersey, and the Mersey and Irwell Canal pass. Shortly after leaving the viaduct the town of Warrington is seen on the E., and westward lies Penketh, and the small white buildings at Fiddler's Ferry.

WARRINGTON STATION.

Distance to Birmingham, 78—Liverpool and Manchester, 19½ miles.

DISTANCES BY ROADS FROM THIS STATION TO THE FOLLOWING PLACES:—

Place E. of Station.		
Grappenhall	3½	miles.
Lymm	5½	—
Warburton	8	—
Bowdon	11¾	—
ALTRINGHAM	12	—

WARRINGTON forms a pleasing view from the approaching trains.

It contains 19,155 inhabitants, and is by some writers supposed to have been originally a British town, and on the invasion of the Romans under Agricola, in 79, to have been converted into a Roman station. This supposition rests chiefly on the circumstances of three Roman roads tending hitherwards to a ford over the Mersey; the vestiges of a castrum and fosse, still discernable; and the discovery of Roman coins and other relics near the ford.

On its occupation by the Saxons, it obtained the name of *Wering-tun*, from *Wæring*, a fortification, and *tun*, a town. The river was passed by ford till 1496, when Thomas, first Earl of Derby, erected a stone bridge in compliment to Henry VII., when on his visit to Latham and Knowsley. In the reign of Henry VIII., Leland, speaking of Warrington, says, "It is a pavid towne of prety bignes, the paroche chirce is at the tayle of the towne; it is a better market than Manchestre." In the civil wars of 1643, the Royalists of the place betook themselves to the *church*, which they fortified, but the Parliamentarian battery dislodged them from their military sanctuary. The town is pleasantly situated on the Mersey; the streets are chiefly narrow, but contain some good buildings.

Prior to the construction of the railroad between Liverpool and Manchester, seventy stage-coaches passed through Warrington daily; now only *four* run. The manufactures comprise muslin, calico, velveteen, sailcloth, (which was formerly the staple trade,) pins, files, hardware, glass, malt, soap, and ale of strength and quality renowned. Railways, rivers, and canals, facilitate trade materially. The market days are Wednesday and Saturday; the fairs commence July 18 and November 30, continuing ten days. There are cloth halls, and various public buildings, and a fine old church, dedicated to St. Helen; the architecture exhibits traces of various styles and periods. Two ancient sepulchral chapels remain, and contain some magnificent monuments of the Boteler, Massey, and Patten families. There are two other churches, and various dissenting chapels and meetings, Free Grammar School, Blue Coat School, and many others, also Hospitals and other excellent institutions.

CHAPTER VIII.

WARRINGTON TO NEWTON JUNCTION,

Four and ¾ Miles.

PASSING on from Warrington, the line commands a view W. of Busey Hall, (seat of Lord Lilford,) a fine old mansion, surrounded by wood; a little farther, is Burton Wood and Bold Heath and Park, (seat of Sir Henry Houghton,) also on the W., Orford Hall (seat of Hon. Mrs. Hornby) on the E., and Billinge Beacon Hill N.W. The spire of Winwick Church is seen shortly before arriving at

Winwick Station,

which, though not mentioned in the Company's list, has, since the opening of the railway, been used as a station, for the accommodation of persons in the vicinity.

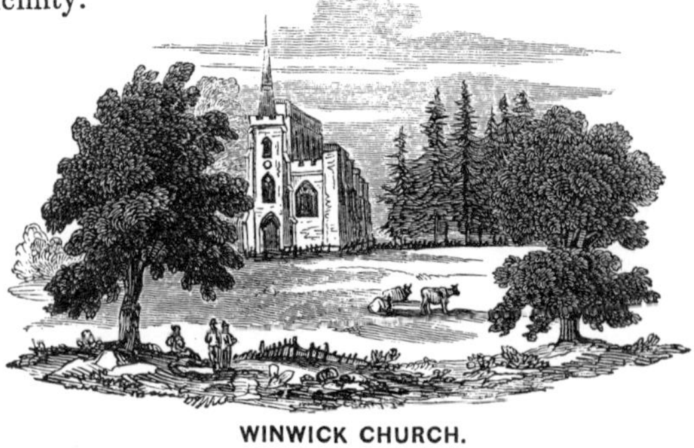

WINWICK CHURCH.

Winwick Church

Winwick Church is a beautiful and ancient edifice, with a lofty spire; and is said to be coeval with the establishment of the Christian religion in this country.

Winwick Hall, residence of the Rector and Lord of the Manor, the Rev. J. J. Hornby, is near the church. This living is one of the wealthiest in the kingdom. Between the village of Winwick and town of Newton, is an elevated piece of ground, called Red Bank, from its having been, in 1648, the scene of a battle between Oliver Cromwell and the Scots, when the latter were defeated with great slaughter.

A short distance brings us to the

Newton Junction.

CHAPTER IX.

NEWTON JUNCTION TO LIVERPOOL.

Fourteen and ¾ Miles.

HAVING to describe the railroad branches to Liverpool and Manchester, we shall now continue our account along the Liverpool part of the line, and in the next Chapter take the "Newton to Manchester" portion. Leaving the Newton Junction, and turning to the left, the E. becomes North, and the W. we must call South. The constant traffic on the Liverpool and Manchester line, and the numerous trains journeying to and fro, render it a much more busy and stirring scene than the Birmingham railroad is at present.

The Grand Junction Company rent the use of this Liverpool and Manchester railway at 20,000 per annum. The exact length of the Liverpool and Manchester railway, from the station, Lime-street, Liverpool, to Water-street, Manchester, is thirty miles and three quarters, and thirty yards.

A short distance from the Junction is the Sankey Viaduct, a grand and stupendous work; the arches are nine in number, and fifty feet span; the embankments leading to and from it, are from sixty to eighty feet above the level country. Newton Common and Race-ground, the stand on which is a conspicuous object, lie to the N., with the Billinge hills behind, Burton Wood S., and the Sankey Canal winds along from either side. After passing

Collin's Green Station

Bold Hall (seat of Sir Henry Houghton) appears to the S., and we soon enter on the Parr Moss, passing the Sutton copper works on the N.

St. Helen's and Runcorn Junction Station.

Here the St. Helen's line branches to the N., and the Runcorn Gap Railway, S. Shirley Hall lies on the N. side. On the S., is the Engine-house, where an engine is stationed to assist trains in ascending the Sutton inclined plane. Proceeding through the Sutton cutting, and under several fine arches, the

Lea Green Station, (top of Sutton incline,)

at the summit of the elevation, is gained, and Rainhill level entered upon. The village of Sutton and Grove Hall are nearly hidden from view by the surrounding trees.

Kendrick's Cross Station, Rainhill.

From Rainhill station the line passes through a short cutting, and then descends the Whiston inclined plane.

Prescot Church is on the N. side, with Ellsby Hills and Halton Castle on the S.

PRESCOT TOWN AND CHURCH.

The town of Prescot, one mile N. of the line, lies principally on a substratum of coal, several mines of which are excavated to its very edge. The district has long been noted for the superior construction of watch tools and motion-work. The drawing of pinion-wire originated here; and small files, considered to be of great excellence, are made and exported in large quantities. Coarse earthenware, especially sugar moulds, are here made from the clay of the neighbourhood, which is particularly adapted to the purpose. The plate-glass works at Ravenhead are very extensive and celebrated. The concave and convex mirrors, and large plate-glass, being equal, if not superior to any produced on the Continent. The Church is ancient; the spire, which was rebuilt in 1789, is 156 feet high, and is a fine object from the railroad. In the Church are several monuments, one by Sir Francis Chantrey, R.A., is of great beauty. John Philip Kemble, the tragedian, was born at Prescot, in 1757. The view of the Cheshire hills in the southward distance, is rich and extensive.

Knowsley Park, seat of the Earl of Derby, appears on the N. The mansion has evidently been erected at different periods; its most ancient part is of stone, and is said to have been raised by the first Earl of Derby, for the reception of his son-in-law, King Henry VII., in whose honours the Earl had been mainly instrumental. Great enlargement and decoration of the mansion took place on occasion of this royal visit: a handsome stone bridge was thrown across the Mersey at Warrington, and an embankment or causeway thrown up across the marshes to the rising ground on the Cheshire side. Many valuable and interesting pictures adorn the mansion, which is surrounded by a beautiful park.

Several coal, lime, and marble works are passed on either side; and while traversing the Huyton embankment, Preston church, the Hazels, seat of Joseph Birch, Esq., and the church and village of Huyton are observed on the N. On the S. appears Childwall park, hall, and church; beyond, is Woolton hall, seat of N. Ashton, Esq.; the whole scene finely wooded.

Huyton Gate and Roby-lane Gate Stations

are shortly passed; the village of Roby lies S. of the line, and closely adjoining it. Proceeding onwards, along a pleasant but not very interesting part, Summerhill house is seen, the seat of Thomas Case, Esq.; also, the little church of Notting Ash and Childwall hall, a seat of the Marquis of Salisbury.

Broad Green Station.

A FEW yards from the station, on the N. side, is a place for the landing of cattle, sheep, &c. The line now enters the Olive Mount excavation, which is an immense chasm, cut in the solid rock, to the depth of from 50 to 70 feet, the precipitous rock forming a grand wall on either side. The village of Wavertree lies S. of the line, after emerging from the Olive Mount ravine; Spekelands, the residence of Mrs. Earle, lies also on the S., and on the N. is the residence of C. Lawrence, Esq. Here the Liverpool tunnels commence; one, for conveying passengers, &c., into the Company's station-yard in Lime-street, turns off on the right hand, and is 2,230 yards long, 25 feet wide, and 17 feet high. The other, for the conveyance of goods, direct to the docks, in a straighter continuation of the line, is 2,250 yards long, 22 feet wide, and 16 feet high. Engines are stationed on each side of the line at this part, each of forty-horse power, to draw the trains up the inclined plane of the tunnel, in coming out of Liverpool, and let them down on their arrival from Birmingham. The locomotive engines being attached to and detached from the trains at this station.

"A Friend to Railways," in a letter to the Editor of the Railway Magazine, May 1838, thus describes the mode of drawing the trains up the inclined plane:—

"At the upper end of the tunnel, which is 2,250 yards long, there is one pair of engines on each side of the road; it being found that a much more regular motion is given by this means to the carriages. The engines are high-pressure, with side-levers, similar to marine engines; the connecting-rods, however, are reversed, and work the crank downwards, and are connected to a horizontal shaft of great strength running across and under the road in a tunnel, upon which shaft a large drum-wheel is placed that works the rope. In each engine-house is a raised platform, upon which the man stands who works the engines; this platform leads to a balcony on the outside of the engine-house, from which the man can look down the mouth of the tunnel; a signal is given by means of an air-pipe running through the tunnel, so formed at the upper end as to produce a sound when the air is forced into it from the lower extremity. This, I believe, is the invention of Mr. King, of Liverpool. The engine-man on hearing the signal, opens the steam-cock, and the engines start instantly. This work was designed by Mr. Grantham, of the foundery of Messrs. Mather and Dickson, of Liverpool, where the machinery was constructed."

Having now given an account of the whole journey, we must proceed to a brief history and memoir of Liverpool itself.

CHAPTER X.

LIVERPOOL.

LIVERPOOL is an ancient sea-port, borough, and market town, 205 miles from London, containing 205,964 inhabitants, exclusive of 10,000 seamen.

Of its remote antiquity but little can be asserted, amidst the great contrariety of opinion which is held on this subject. Liverpool is not noticed in any of the Roman Itinera, neither does the name occur in the Norman survey. After the conquest it was granted by William, to Roger de Poictiers, together with all the land between the Ribble and the Mersey, and subsequently forfeited. It was thereupon granted to the Earls of Chester; and on forfeiture by their descendants, to Edmund, son of Henry III., as parcel of the honour of Lancaster; and it remained an integral part of the duchy possessions, until its alienation by Charles I., in 1628.

Various opinions have been hazarded regarding the etymology of the name, without reference to the most ancient documents in which it has been discovered. John, whilst Earl of Moreton, and in possession of the honour of Lancaster, confirmed a grant made by his father, Henry II., to Warin de Lancaster, of *Liverpul*, with other places, under a certain *reddendum*. In subsequent records it is written *Lyrpul*, *Lythyrpul*, &c., signifying, probably, in the ancient dialect of this country, the "lower pool." Some deduce its etymology from a pool frequented by an aquatic fowl, called a "Liver," or from a sea-weed of that name; others, and with much more reason, from the ancient British word *Lir*, "the sea," and a spreading water or pool, viz., the sea pool, or sea-water pool.

Camden says the Castle was built by Roger de Poictiers, in 1089; it certainly was erected at a very early period. In October, 1323, Edward II. dates his orders, &c., from Liverpool Castle; and in April, 1358, Henry, Duke of Lancaster, resided there for a month. It was demolished by order of Parliament, during the commonwealth, and in 1715, its site was granted by Queen Anne, to the corporation, who built St. George's Church upon it. On King John ascending the throne, at his brother's death, he again came into possession of the honour of Lancaster, and granted a charter to the town of Liverpool, which Henry III., in 1229, confirmed, made the town a free borough, instituted a guild merchant, and granted additional privileges. These charters have been confirmed, and further ones granted by succeeding sovereigns. The several mandates for fitting-out and providing vessels for the royal service, addressed by Edward II. and III., and subsequent kings, afford proof of its then being a place of extensive trade at this early period; and the fact of the royal order for the prohibition of the export of grain, in the time of Richard III., being transmitted to Liverpool only, is also a proof of its then being the only shipping port in the country. Leland, in 1558, described it thus: "*Lyrpole*, alias *Lyrpoole*, a pavid towne, hath but a chapel, Walton, a iiii miles off, not far from the se, is paroche chirche. The king hath a castell there, and the Earle of Darbe hath a stone house there. Irisch marchants cum much thither, as to a good haven. After that Mersey water cumming towards Runcorne in Cheshire liseth among the commune people the name, and is Lyrpole. At Lyrpole is smaule costume payid that causith merchants to resorte. Good marchaundis at Lyrpole, and much Irisch yarn that Manchester men do by ther." Liverpool appears to have declined, probably from the baneful influences of the wars of York and Lancaster, until the latter part of the reign of Elizabeth, when, in a petition from the inhabitants to the Queen, it is described as "Her Majesty's poor decayed town of Liverpool." Its poverty may be understood from the fact, that when Charles I. levied his iniquitous and despotic tax of ship money, this town was rated at £26 only, while Bristol was rated at £1,000. In the civil war Liverpool was alternately held by the Parliamentarians, taken by Prince Rupert, and retaken by the Parliament. In the reign of William III., that monarch, with part of his train, embarked at this port for Ireland, previously to the battle of the Boyne; and regiments and privateer vessels were here equipped against the Pretender and the French.

Times and manners are somewhat changed here since 1617, when one of the orders of the common-council demanded, "that every council-man shall come to council *clean-shaved*, and in his long clothes." Slander and gossip were very severely punished by the civic dignitaries, it being a law, "that if any man speak ill of the mayor, he shall lose his freedom."

The most important feature in the history of this place, is the extraordinary rapidity with which it has risen into a degree of splendour and importance, without example in the history of any commercial country. Among the causes which have produced its elevation to a rank but partially inferior to the metropolis, are, its situation on the shore of a noble river, which expands into a wide estuary; its proximity to the Irish coast; its central position with respect to the United Kingdom; its intimate connexion with the principal manufacturing districts, and with every part of the kingdom, by numerous rivers, canals, and railroads, and the persevering industry and enterprising spirit of its inhabitants. Without the romance, we may see among them the reality,of the merchant-nobles of Genoa and Venice; and the grandeur which pervades the modern buildings of our English port may scarcely be outvied in stateliness, and certainly not in fitness and utility, by any palace-city of the past.

As we passed along the busy quays of these crowded docks, and thought of the wealth conveyed by the winged couriers of the ocean there congregated, the following gorgeous lines in Marlow's Jew of Malta, occurred to us: perhaps the expectant owners of argosies bound hitherward, deal not quite so largely as the poet's Crœsus, in jewelled treasures; but we cannot very honestly change amethysts into tobacco, nor bags of fiery opals into bales of cotton wool; the circumstances of the case may therefore be allowed to vary a little, without our transposing the terms:—

"As for those Samnites, and the men of Uzz,
That bought my Spanish oils, and wines of Greece,
Here have I purst their paltry silverlings,
Fie! what a trouble 'tis to count this trash!
Give me the merchants of the Indian mines,
That trade in metal of the purest gold;
The wealthy Moor, that in the eastern rocks
Without control can pick his riches up,
And in his house keep pearls like pebble stones;
Receive them free, and sell them by the weight:
Bags of fiery opals, sapphires, amethysts,
Jacinths, hard topaz, grass-green emeralds,
Beauteous rubies, sparkling diamonds,
And seld' seen costly stones of so great price,
As one of them, indifferently rated,
And of a caract of this quality
May serve, in peril of calamity
To rescue great kings from captivity.
This is the ware wherein consists my wealth,
And thus methinks, should men of judgment frame
Their means of traffic from the vulgar trade,
And as their wealth increaseth, so inclose
Infinite riches in a little room.
But now—how stands the wind?
Into what corner peers my halcyon's bill?
Ha! to east? yes:—see how stands the vane?
East and by south, why then I hope my ships
I sent from Egypt, and the bordering isles,
Are gotten up by Nilus' winding banks:
Mine argosies from Alexandria,
Loaden with spice and silks, now under sail
Are smoothly gliding down by Candy shore
To Malta, through our Mediterranean sea."

We have, ere this, noted many a merchant (not of Venice) to whom we have mentally applied Salarino's words to Antonio; and few will grudge the space we here occupy, by a quotation so apt and beautiful:—

"*Salarino.* Your mind is tossing on the ocean;
There, where your argosies with portly sail,
Like seigniors and rich burghers of the flood,
Or, as it were, the pageants of the sea,—
Do overpeer the petty traffickers,
That curtsey to them, do them reverence,
As they fly by them with their woven wings.
——My wind, cooling my broth,
Would blow me to an ague, when I thought
What harm a wind too great might do at sea.
I should not see the sandy hour-glass run,
But I should think of shallows and of flats,
And see my wealthy Andrew docked in sand,
Vailing her high-top lower than her ribs,
To kiss her burial. Should I go to church,
And see the holy edifice of stone,
And not bethink me straight of dangerous rocks?
Which touching but my gentle vessel's side,
Would scatter all her spices on the stream,
Enrobe the rolling waters with my silks,
And, in a word, but even now worth this,
And now worth nothing. Shall I have the thought
To think on this; and shall I lack the thought
That such a thing be-chanced, would make me sad?
But, tell not me; I know, Antonio
Is sad to think upon his merchandise.
Antonio. Believe me, No; I thank my fortune for it,
My ventures are not in one bottom trusted,
Nor to one place: nor is my whole estate
Upon the fortune of this present year:
Therefore my merchandise makes me not sad."

SHAKSPEARE.

The commerce of the port may be divided into three branches: first, the trade with Ireland, whence a variety of produce, chiefly grain, cattle, &c., is imported, the gross value of which has amounted annually to £4,497,708, exclusive of linen and manufactured wares. Liverpool enjoys about two-fifths of the Irish trade. The chief exports are British manufactured goods, salt, coal, and general merchandise. The second principal branch of trade is that with the United States of America, of which it engrosses more than three-fourths of the whole commerce of the kingdom. The chief import is cotton wool, and from this port Manchester and the manufacturing districts are supplied with the raw material. Tobacco is also imported to an *alarming* extent. The average quantity annually introduced for the contamination of our atmosphere, being 7,623 *hogsheads*—what a fearful store of materials for smoking the brains, and dusting the nostrils of our fellow-creatures! A great quantity of American flour is also imported. The third branch of the trade is that with the West Indies, which commenced about the middle of the seventeenth century, and which was previously engrossed by London and Bristol. Sugar, rum, and coffee, are the chief luxuries we receive thence through the other ports. The trade with the East Indies is smaller; the imports are cotton, indigo, hides, ginger, pepper, and sugar. With the ports of the Mediterranean and Levant seas, Liverpool has considerable traffic, importing wine, fruits, lemon and lime juice, olive and other oils, barilla, and brimstone. From Egypt is brought cotton; and from the Baltic sea-ports, timber, tallow, &c. The gross receipts of the customs at this port alone, exceed the sum derived from the nine other principal ports of the three kingdoms (London excepted), viz., Bristol, Hull, Newcastle, Leith, Glasgow, Grenock, Dublin, Belfast, and Cork. Vessels from, and bound to, all parts of the globe, are congregated here; and there is scarcely a place in the world accessible to the British flag, to which a ready conveyance is not afforded from this enterprising port.

The harbour is capacious and secure: at the entrance of the river is the Black Rock Lighthouse, erected on a point of rock on the western coast. A floating light is also placed eleven miles seaward from the mouth of the river.

For the security of the shipping in the port, and for

the greater facility of loading and unloading merchandise, immense ranges of docks and warehouses, extending upwards of two miles along the eastern bank of the river, have been constructed, on a scale of unparalleled magnificence; and forming one of those characteristics of commercial greatness in which this town is unrivalled. The docks are of three kinds:—the wet docks, which are chiefly for ships of great burden, employed in the foreign trade, and which float in them at all states of the tide, the water being retained by gates; the dry docks, so called because they are left dry when the tide is out, are chiefly appropriated to coasting vessels; and the graving docks, which admit or exclude the water at pleasure, are adapted to the repair of ships, during which they are kept dry, and when completed are floated out by admitting the tide. The Canning Dock is chiefly occupied by sloops from the north coast, which import corn, provisions, and slate, and convey back the produce of the Mediterranean, the West Indies, Portugal, and the Baltic: it has a quay 500 yards in length. The Salthouse Dock is for vessels in the Levant, Irish, and coasting trades: the quay is 759 yards in extent. George's Dock has a quay 1001 yards in length. The King's Dock is appropriated to vessels from Virginia and other parts, laden with tobacco; which article is exclusively landed here, and occupies a range of warehouses 575 feet in length, and 239 in depth. The Queen's Dock, 470 yards long, with a spacious quay, is chiefly occupied by vessels freighted with timber, and by those employed in the Dutch and Baltic trades. The Brunswick Dock is larger than any of the preceding, and receives vessels laden with timber. Prince's Dock is 500 yards in length, with spacious quays, and along the west side is a beautiful marine parade, 750 yards long, and eleven wide, defended by a stone parapet wall, from which is a delightful view of the river and the shipping: it is much frequented as a promenade. To the westward of these are the Clarence Dock and Basin, appropriated solely to the use of the steam vessels trading to and from the port: there are several smaller docks, and considerable additions are contemplated. When these are completed, the whole range of docks will be two miles and 820 yards in length, exclusively of the openings to the several docks: the total area of water space contained in them is upwards of ninety statute acres, and the extent of the quays in lineal measure is 12,511 yards, or upwards of seven miles; yet spacious as they are, they are still considered inadequate to the increasing commerce of the port. Several ranges of commodious baths are situated in the vicinity of the docks; there are hot, cold, floating, and medicated vapour baths.

The new Custom-house is a superb and beautiful edifice, in the Grecian style of architecture, 454 feet in length, 224 in depth, with three principal fronts of great magnificence. The Exchange buildings, erected by the late Mr. John Forster, form sides of a quadrangular area, in the centre of which is a monument to the memory of Lord Nelson. The north front of the Hall forms the fourth side of this square. This is a stately and magnificent structure in the Grecian style, with four elegant fronts, and contains on the ground floor a council-room, and apartments for the mayor, town clerk, pensioners, and corporation. The grand staircase leads into a spacious saloon, splendidly decorated with royal portraits by Lawrence, Hopner, Phillips, &c. Two spacious ball-rooms, and two richly furnished drawing rooms, decorated with marble pillars, chandeliers, &c., are entered from the saloon. A grand banquet-room, refectory, &c., &c., fitted up with great taste and splendour, are also comprised in this grand suit of apartments. The Public Subscription Libraries are numerous and well selected. The Athenæum contains a news-room and an extensive library. The Lyceum is a handsome edifice of the Ionic order; contains a library, coffee-room, lecture, and committee-rooms. The Union News-room, Exchange News-room, Medical and Law Libraries, are all well supported. The Royal Institution is a spacious and handsome edifice, containing on the ground floor, lecture, reading, and school-rooms; on the first floor, a large room for the Literary and Philosophical Society, a library, museum, spacious exhibition rooms for the Liverpool Academy of painting, &c. On the roof is an observatory, and behind are a laboratory and a theatre for chemical and philosophical experiments. This institution was formed in 1814, for the advancement of literature, science, and the arts; and the members were incorporated by royal charter, in 1822. Professors, lecturers, and masters are appointed by the society. The Botanic Gardens near Edge Hill, and the Zoological Gardens, are valuable additions to the rational and profitable amusements of the inhabitants. There is a Theatre, Amphitheatre, and Circus, the former for the drama, the two latter for equestrian performances and pantomimes. The Wellington Rooms, for balls, are admirably adapted for such gay scenes. The summer races in July continue four days, the course lies five miles to the N.E. of the town. The grand stand is capable of accommodating 2,000 persons. The chartered market days are Wednesday and Saturday, and for corn, Tuesday and Friday. The Market-houses are numerous, handsome, and commodious.

The corporation of Liverpool have an income of above £100,000 per annum, a great portion of which is expended in the improvement of the port and embellishment of the town. The Churches of the Establishment are about twenty-four in number, some of them of great architectural beauty. In addition to the Churchyards, there are two extensive Cemeteries, one near Edge-hill; the other occupying a large tract of ground, excavated as a quarry for stone used in the building of the docks, and converted into a depository for the dead, at an expense of £21,000; it is tastefully laid out, and has a suitable chapel for the performance of the funeral service. The buildings dedicated to religious purposes by the several sects of Dissenters, are about forty in number, some of them of considerable beauty. The Public Schools are very numerous, and so well supported as to render them valuably and most extensively useful. That for the indigent blind, was established in 1791; 120 pupils now receive instruction in various branches, and are taught spinning, basket-making, the weaving of linen, sacking, carpeting, the making of list shoes, twine, worsted rugs, and other trades, by which they may earn a livelihood; they are also instructed in music. Asylums and Institutions, too numerous to be here enumerated; Hospitals, Infirmaries ; Societies for the assistance and relief of aged seamen, and other humane and admirable purposes, are, by the munificence of the inhabitants, all enabled to administer in no small degree to the wants and misfortunes of suffering fellow-beings.

Among the distinguished natives of the town may be noticed Jeremiah Horrox, the astronomer, born 1619, at Toxteth Park, near Liverpool. He is supposed to have been the first person who ever predicted or observed the transit of Venus over the sun's disk. He died on the 3rd of January, 1641, a few days after completing his treatise on the transit which took place in the November preceding. George Stubbs, the animal painter, born 1724. William Sadler, who invented the application of copper-plate prints to the embellishment of earthenware. William Roscoe, author of the lives of Lorenzo de Medici, and of Leo X. He died in 1831, aged seventy-nine, equally beloved and regretted for his excellence as a man, and for his ability as an author. The Rev. William Shepherd, author of the life of Poggio Brachiolini, &c., an elegant writer, and earnest reformer. Dr. Currie, the intelligent biographer of Burns, was also a native of Liverpool, as was the gentle-minded and truly feminine poet, Felicia Hemans.

The manufactures of Liverpool, are chiefly such as

are connected with the port and the shipping, the promotion of its commerce, and the supply of its inhabitants. There are several very large sugar refineries, extensive potteries, glass-houses, breweries, tanneries, salt and copperas works, iron and brass foundries, foundries for cannon, anchors, chain-cables, and steam engine machinery, manufactories for steam-boilers, engines, also guns, small arms, sails, cordage, watches, tobacco, snuff, and soap. There are numerous mills for grinding corn, mustard, colours, and dye-woods: the manufacture of soap exceeds that of any place in England. The average number of watches made annually, is 11,500, a number greater than any town, except London. Ship-building is carried on to a great extent; several men-of-war have been launched from the dock-yards; and in the building of steam vessels, Liverpool takes the lead of all other ports. The trade of the town is greatly facilitated by the extensive inland navigation in every direction, by which it is connected with the manufacturing districts and chief towns in the kingdom. No less than five water conveyances fall into the Mersey, viz., the Mersey and Irwell Navigation, Duke of Bridgewater's Canal, Sankey Canal, Chester and Ellesmere Canal, and Weaver Navigation, opening communication with Manchester, Bolton, Hull, South Lancashire, Birmingham, Worcestershire, South of England, and Wales.

The information required by the traveller respecting inns, coach-offices, &c., will be found in the Appendix; together with a list of places of amusement and interest, worthy the attention of a stranger in this great and truly splendid sea-port.

CHAPTER XI.

NEWTON JUNCTION TO MANCHESTER,

Fourteen and $\frac{3}{4}$ Miles.

On leaving the Newton (or, as it is called in the neighbourhood, Warrington) Junction, the neat little town of Newton is seen N. of the line, not far from the Legh Arms Hotel, a comfortable and reasonable house.

TOWN OF NEWTON.

Opposite, lying S. of the line, we again see the spire of Winwick Church, Mow Copp, and the Cheshire and Rivington hills appear in the distance.

Park Side Station.

Here the machine and apparatus for supplying the engines with fuel and water is well worth observing, though with great caution, as there are five lines of rails in this place; and the difficulty of escaping from a coming train is no small one to a stranger, who, standing upon, or among them, would find himself greatly bewildered in any emergency. The horrible death of Mr. Huskisson, from the injuries he received at this very spot, may be a salutary warning to the adventurous. A white marble slab in the wall commemorates the awful event, which it is useless to allude to further, the particulars being so well known. The Wigan Junction Line branches off a short distance from this point. Passing a short cutting on Highfield Moor, we reach the most considerable one on the Manchester and Liverpool line, the Kenyon excavation, the materials taken from which contributed mainly towards the adjacent embankments. The Bolton Junction line turns N. from this part, at which is

The Bolton Junction Station.

We now enter on the Brossley embankment, and observe Culcheth Hall, S., and Hurst Hall, N. of the line; the former the residence of T. E. Withington, Esq., the latter of T. Molineux Steel, Esq.

Bury-Lane Station

closely adjoins the Chat Moss tavern, near which the

line crosses the little stream Glazebrook. S. is a farm-house, called Light Oats Hall. Here commences an embankment planted with trees; passing which we enter on the famed Chat Moss, formerly a barren and cultureless waste; but at length yielding to agricultural skill and industry, several portions having already been drained and successfully cultivated.

CHAT MOSS.

The road traverses this immense bog for a distance of four miles and three quarters. S. of the line is a fine view of the Cheshire and Derbyshire hills, with the village of Astley and Tildsley Church spire. Rivington Pike, and the Billinge Beacon lie on the N., and the Chat Moss all around. Immense labour and perseverance were required to achieve the great work of forming a firm and durable road over this swampy tract, which varies in depth from ten to above thirty feet.

Several neat habitations are now erected on the farm-lands redeemed from the swamp: of these, Barton Moss Farm is the chief. N. of the Moss lies Worsley Hall, seen from the line, on an eminence. Botany Bay, a place of singularly ill-omened name, is also on the left, or N. side. The hills before mentioned still form the back ground of the views on either side. Leaving the Chat Moss by the Barton embankment, the line passes

Patricroft Station;

Near to this are large iron foundries and silk works. The Bridgewater Canal passes under, and the turnpike-road over, the line. Monton Church and village appear N. of the road; and shortly after, the village and Church of Eccles are seen on the S.

ECCLES CHURCH.

This small place has achieved fame by two means: the death of Mr. Huskisson, which took place at the house of the Rev. Mr. Blackburn; and by its cakes, which the traveller is invited to purchase by a board over the door of a house close by the station, on which is inscribed, "This is the noted Eccles cake shop." Passing

Waste Lane Station

some cottages and factories, and the city of chimneys, Manchester, appear in view. The village of Tinker's Hollow, and

Cross Lane Bridge Station

being passed, also sundry arches and bridges across the river Irwell, and the engine, trains, and travellers, are received into the Company's yard in Manchester.

CHAPTER XII.

MANCHESTER.

THE town of Manchester, including Salford, contains 270,960 inhabitants, and is distant from London 186 miles, and from Liverpool thirty-one by the railroad.

The origin of this town, which is remarkable for the extent of its trade, and the importance of its manufactures, may be traced to remote antiquity. In the time of the Druids, it was distinguished as one of the principal stations of their priests, and celebrated for the privilege of sanctuary attached to its altar, which, in the British language, was called *Meyne*, signifying a stone. Prior to the Christian era, it was one of the principal seats of the Brigantes, who had a castle or stronghold, called *Mancenion*, or the place of tents, near the confluence of the rivers Medlock and Irwell, the site of which, still called the "Castle Field," was selected as a station by the Romans, on their conquest of this part of Britain under Agricola, about the year 79, and called by them *Mancunium*, whence the Saxon *Manceastre*, and our *Manchester*. The Romans occupied this station during nearly four centuries, and formed roads, branching off to their surrounding settlements. Various antiquities have been from time to time discovered in the neighbourhood. After the departure of the Romans, a party of Saxons took the fort from the Britons, to whom the garrison afterwards surrendered. In 620, it was captured by Edwin, King of Northumbria. In 627, the inhabitants were converted to Christianity, by Paulinus, a missionary from Gregory I. Manchester having been taken by the Danes, was wrested from their possession, about 920, by Edward the Elder, who rebuilt and fortified the town and castle. For some time it continued prosperous, but suffered greatly in the wars between the Danes and Northumbrians. The early history of all ancient towns, chiefly "pertains to feats of broils and battles;" castles founded, demolished, and rebuilt, to be destroyed again; baronial feuds and fierce invasions; with the faint and fruitless struggles of *right* against *might*, make up the dark and bloody record.

After the twelfth century, a calmer period arrived; and, though occasionally troubled by the pest of war, the fortunes of the now wealthy town of Manchester, have been progressively increasing. From the year 1352, we may date the commencement of its manufacturing celebrity, when a kind of woollen cloth, made from the fleece, in an unprepared state, called "Manchester cotton," was introduced; and some Flemish artisans, invited into England, by Edward III., settled in the town, and brought the woollen manufacture to a considerable degree of perfection. At the time of the Reformation, an ecclesiastical commission was established at Manchester, and exercised great intolerance, imprisoning and executing numbers of popish recusants; another of the black and by-gone deeds of our past "dark ages." During the Parliamentary war, the head-quarters of the Parliamentarian army, in Lancashire, were fixed at Manchester, which was fortified and defended too well for the Royalist forces to be successful in any of their repeated attacks. In 1652, the walls were thrown down, the fortifications demolished, and the gates carried away and sold. The good town of Manchester had grown great and wealthy; but we much doubt if it had become particularly grave or wise, since we know that extravagant rejoicings, accompanied by every splendour of pomp and ceremony, took place at the restoration of the not-too-excellent King Charles II., in whose honour, and to the glorification of the thirsty woollen-weavers, the public conduits flowed with streams of wine, instead of water; a celebration worthy of the "merry monarch."

In 1745, Prince Charles Edward entered Manchester with his army, and took up his abode in the house of Mr. Dickenson, in

Market-street, when he levied money, raised men and horses for his service, and after marching about the country, made a rapid retreat into Scotland, before the army of the Duke of Cumberland. The officers of the Manchester regiment, were tried for high treason, and executed on Kennington Common, two of the heads being placed on Temple Bar, and two on the Exchange, Manchester. With this inhuman and disgraceful event, the record of the "fortunes of war," connected with this place, ends,—we will trust for ever.

The various manufactures carried on in Manchester, would occupy a descriptive work of no small extent, in themselves; and the account which so small a volume as the present can find space for, must be brief indeed. The staple trade is the cotton manufacture, which, in all its branches, is carried on to an almost incredible extent. From the time of Edward III., when the "Manchester cottons" were first introduced, this branch of trade has been increasing in importance. About the year 1740, cotton was manufactured by the spindle and distaff in the cottages of the workmen, chiefly into fustians, thicksets, dimities, and jeans, to which other kinds of goods were shortly added. About the year 1760, these goods, hitherto made only for home consumption, formed a market on the continent of Europe and America, and in consequence of the increased demand, recourse was had to the aid of machinery. The spinning jennies, invented by Messrs. Kay and Highs, have been introduced, and greatly improved by Mr. Hargreaves, whose success, exciting the apprehensions of the hand-workmen, caused the destruction of his machinery, and his retreat to Nottingham, where he died in indigence. Sir Richard Arkwright, the late Sir Robert Peel, and others, have improved and invented other machines, which, aided by the power of the steam-engine, have prodigiously increased the quantity and variety of the goods manufactured in this town.

In the spinning department alone, there are in the town and vicinity 114 factories, worked by 118 steam-engines, the aggregate power of which is equal to that of 3,981 horses; by this machinery, 2,182,350 spindles, and 6,926 power-looms are set in motion. The power-looms, a recent invention, originating with the Rev. Mr. Cartwright, of Holland House, Kent, were not proved finally successful till 1806. The factories, in several of which the whole process of the manufacture, from the introduction of the raw material, to the completion of the fabric, is carried on, are immense ranges of building, from six to eight stories in height, some employing 2,000 persons each, and the whole affording employment to upwards of 30,000 persons. The principal articles at present manufactured are velvets, fustians, jeans, ticking, checks, ginghams, nankeens, diaper, quilting, calico, muslins, muslinets, cambric handkerchiefs, small wares, silks, and, in fact, every variety of cotton and silk goods. There are also extensive bleaching grounds, works for printing and dyeing, and all other departments of the manufacture. Extensive forges, foundries, &c., for the machinery used, laboratories for chemical productions used in the trade, and mills for the manufacture of all descriptions of paper; engraving, as connected with the printing of cotton and muslin goods, is carried on to a great extent; and there are hat manufactories, and saw mills on a very large scale. It is needless to inform the reader, that an inspection of some of these immense hives of labour and invention, will well repay the trouble of a visit. It is a proud feeling to an Englishman to know, that the productions of the thousand busy hands and whirling wheels around him, are destined to increase the comfort, refinement, or splendour of nations, spread far and wide over the globe: and it is a joyful thing to compare present greatness and secure freedom, with the long past years when a little bristling fortress and a tented field, scenes of barbaric bloodshed and grovelling slavery, occupied the spot of earth now devoted to usefulness, industry, and knowledge.

Manchester is situated on the banks of the river Irwell; (which here receives the tributary streams of the Irk and the Medlock;) on the N.W. bank lies the newly erected borough of Salford, connected by means of five bridges with Manchester, of which it forms an integral part. In various parts of the town there are altogether nearly sixty bridges. The town is well paved, and lighted with gas; and the inhabitants are supplied with water by the Manchester and Salford Water Company. The environs, in many parts, particularly in Broughton, Ardwick-green, and Gibraltar, are pleasant, and present many ranges of handsome residences, tasteful villas, and cottages. In the older parts of the town are several ancient houses, interspersed with modern dwellings, and, except where recent improvements have been made, the streets are inconveniently narrow; the accommodation of trade being more studied here than elegance and symmetry of appearance.

The public buildings and institutions of Manchester are well worthy of its wealth and importance. The Exchange and Commercial Buildings, facing the Market-place, form a spacious handsome edifice, built of Runcorn stone: containing the News-room, Exchange, Library, Post-office, Chamber of Commerce, a spacious Dining-room, and other apartments. The members of the Literary and Philosophical Society have a suitable building for their meetings, and have published many volumes of Transactions in the English, French, and German languages, which are much circulated on the continent. The Royal Institution, embracing a variety of objects connected with literature, science, and the fine arts, has a fine building in the Grecian style, from a design by Mr. Barry, forming a splendid addition to the architectural ornaments of the town. The centre comprises the Hall and Lecture Theatre, lighted by a lantern from the ceiling, which may be darkened instantaneously at the will of the lecturer. One of the wings is appropriated as the Academy of the Fine Arts, with Exhibition-rooms, and the other as a Museum of Natural History. The whole cost of this elegant pile was estimated at £50,000. The Town Hall is a noble edifice, from a design by Mr. F. Goodwin, after the model of the Temple of Erectheus, at Athens, with a beautiful tower and dome in the centre, resembling the Tower of Andronicus, called "The Temple of Winds:" it contains various apartments for transacting the public business of the town, and one splendid room, 132 feet long, decorated with great elegance. The Town Hall at Salford is a handsome and commodious stone edifice by the same architect. The Society for promoting the study of natural history, has a valuable and extensive Museum also; and the town possesses flourishing Mechanics' Institutions, Philological Society, Agricultural Society, Botanic Garden, several Libraries, two Theatres, Assembly-rooms, Concert-rooms, Annual Races, and Triennial Musical Festivals. There are twenty-six churches and chapels belonging to the Establishment, and more than fifty places of worship for the various denominations of Dissenters. The windows of St. John's Church, in Byrom-street, contain some very ancient and beautiful stained glass, brought from a convent in Rouen; also, pictures in the vestry, and a fine piece of sculpture, by Flaxman. The Free Grammar School, founded in the 7th of Henry VIII., has a revenue of £4,000, and the number of scholars is from 150 to 200. The Blue Coat, St. Paul's, Lancasterian, National, and Infants' Schools, are all highly useful, and well-supported establishments; and the various Sunday Schools instruct as many as 30,000 children. The Hospitals and other Charitable Institutions are equally extensive in their sphere of usefulness, and together with the establishments before mentioned, worthy of the wealth, intelligence, and liberality of this great and important town.

Among the distinguished natives of Manchester, or persons who have been otherwise connected with it, may be enumerated, William Crabtree, an astronomical writer, and inventor of the micrometer, born at Broughton, and killed at the battle of Marston Moor in 1644; John Byrom, a poet, and author of a system of shorthand; John Ferriar, M.D., author of Illustrations of Sterne, &c.; Thomas Barritt, the antiquary and heraldist; Thomas Faulkner, an enterprising traveller, who published the earliest account of Patagonia, and died in 1774; the Rev. John Whittaker, the Manchester historian; and others of less renown. Manchester gives the title of duke and earl to the family of Montague. The market days are Tuesday, Thursday, and Saturday; fairs on Easter Monday and Tuesday, and October 1 and 2. Salford fairs begin on Whit Monday, for twenty-one days; and on November 17, for the same time.

The information required by the traveller respecting inns, places of public resort, &c., will be found in the Appendix, under the head Manchester.

END OF THE ROUTE.

BRIDGE.

from this Station to Walsall for the

AMPTON.

from the town meet all the Trains. fnal and Wellington, from the New 8½ a.m.; *Prince of Wales, 12¾ p.m.; the Crown and Cushion:—Salopian, d Ironbridge. To Shrewsbury, from .m., through Shiffnal and Wellington. n.; *6½ p. m. To Bridgenorth, 4 p.m. ot run on Sundays.

ORD.

n attendance to convey passengers to on-on-Trent, Ashby-de-la-Zouch, &c., p.m. Stone and Newcastle, 4½ p.m.

MORE.

Shrewsbury, through Market Drayton. teries daily. The Pottery Company tle and Potteries.

ELEY STATIONS.

in waiting at these Stations to take Potteries, or any other place.

WE.

Macclesfield, through Congleton and A Coach to Whitchurch, daily. An eet all the Trains, and convey passen-

ORD.

s (with the letter bags) to Northwich Mail to Chester and Tarporley, daily. arts of North and South Wales.

BROOK.

Hotel, Runcorn, morning and after- he arrival of the Trains at this station.

GTON.

n attendance to convey passengers to or Gigs, to be had in a few minutes' port, Liverpool, Carlisle, Edinburgh,

RINGTON.

0	Newton Junction.		
	14¾		
6	4 0 3 6	MANCHESTER.	
	14¾	30	
6	4 0 3 6	6 0 4 6	LIVERPOOL

ine, are in proportion to the distance.

rters, or other persons in the

c.—No smoking is allowed in aches, even with the consent of ast may be had at the Station- g by the early train; but no bles of any kind upon the line. he public will co-operate with will be the means of removing nish the chance of accident. ster, or Liverpool, by the even- ly on the following morning.

FARES, TIME, AND DISTANCES, OF THE GRAND JUNCTION RAILWAY COMPANY.

Fares From Birmingham to Liverpool or Manchester. STATIONS.	Gentlemen's Carriages. £. s.	Mail. s. d.	First Class Coach. s. d.	Second Class Coach. s. d.	Time occupied in arriving after starting from Birmingham. 1st Cl. H. M.	Mixed H. M	Distance to Birmingham. Miles.	Horse. £. s.
Birming.								
Perry Barr	..	..	1 6	1 0	..	0 8	3¼	..
Newton Road	..	..	1 6	1 0	..	0 20	6¼	..
Bescot Bridge	..	..	2 0	1 6	..	0 30	9¼	..
James's Bridge	..	..	2 0	1 6	..	0 33	10	..
Willenhall	..	..	2 6	2 0	..	0 46	11¾	..
W'hampton	0 10	3 6	3 0	2 6	0 35	0 56	14¼	0 8
Four Ashes	..	..	4 0	3 0		1 13	20	
Spread Eagle	..	..	4 6	3 6	..	1 17	21½	..
Penkridge	..	..	5 0	4 0	..	1 40	24	..
Stafford	1 0	6 0	6 0	5 0	1 5	1 43	29¼	0 16
Bridgeford	..	..	7 0	5 6	..	1 57	32½	..
Norton Bridge	..	..	7 6	6 0	..	2 9	35	..
Whitmore	1 10	11 0	9 6	8 0	1 45	2 29	43¼	1 1
Madeley	..	..	10 0	8 6	..	2 41	46	..
Basford	..	..	12 0	10 6	..	2 54	51	..
Crewe	1 15	13 6	12 0	10 6	2 14	2 59	54	1 7
Coppenhall	..	..	12 6	10 6	..	3 10	56	..
Minshull Vern.	..	..	13 0	11 0	..	3 18	58¾	..
Winsford	..	..	13 6	11 6	..	3 27	61¼	..
Hartford	2 2	16 6	14 0	12 0	2 49	3 37	65¼	1 13
Acton	..	..	15 0	12 6	..	3 48	68¼	..
Preston Brook	..	..	15 6	13 6	..	4 1	72½	..
Moore	..	..	16 0	14 0	..	4 6	75	..
Warrington	2 10	19 6	17 0	14 0	3 24	4 14	78	1 18
Newton Junct.	..	..	18 0	15 0	..	4 32	82¾	..
Manchester	3 0	23 0	21 0	17 0	4 30	5 15	97¼	2 0
Liverpool	3 0	23 0	21 0	17 0	4 30	5 15	97¼	2 0

The Fare from Birmingham to any Station on the Liverpool and Manchester Line is in proportion.

N.B.—The Mixed Trains also take up and set down Passengers *to or from any part of the Grand Junction Railway*, at all the usual Stopping Places on the Liverpool and Manchester Railway.—An allowance is *included* in the above Tables of five minutes for *all* the Trains at the *principal* Stations, and of three minutes for *the Mixed Trains*, at the intermediate stopping places.—No Fare is less than One Shilling by the principal Trains.—The Fares between the intermediate Stopping Places is at the rate of about 2½d. per mile for First, and 1¾d. for Second Class Passengers. Tables of which are kept at each of the Stations.

Parties arriving at Birmingham by the early Trains, can go on in the same carriage to the London and Birmingham Railway Station, and so proceed by the London Train.

Fares From Liverpool or Manchester to Birmingham. STATIONS.	Gentlemen's Carriages. £. s.	Mail. s. d.	First Class Coach. s. d.	Second Class Coach. s. d.	Time occupied in arriving after starting from Liverpool and Manchester 1st Cl. H. M.	Mixed H. M.	Distance to Liverpool and Manchester. Miles	Horse. £. s.
Liverpool Manchester								
Newton Junct.	..	..	4 0	3 6	..5	0 40	14¾	..
Warrington	0 15	..	4 0	3 6	0 5	0 55	19¼	0 11
Moore	..	..	5 0	4 0	..	1 3	22½	..
Preston Brook	..	..	5 6	4 6	..	1 16	25	..
Acton	..	..	6 0	5 6	..	1 30	29¼	..
Hartford	1 5	8 0	7 0	6 0	1 30	1 40	31¾	0 18
Winsford	..	..	7 6	6 6	..	1 56	36¼	..
Minshull Vern	..	..	8 0	7 0	..	2 2	38¾	..
Coppenhall	..	..	9 0	7 6	..	2 13	41¼	..
Crewe	1 10	11 0	9 6	8 0	2 2	2 23	43¼	1 1
Basford	..	..	11 0	9 6	..	2 40	46¼	..
Madeley	..	..	11 0	9 6	..	2 52	51¼	..
Whitmore	1 15	13 6	12 0	10 0	2 40	3 5	54¼	1 7
Norton Bridge	..	..	13 6	11 6	..	3 28	62¼	..
Bridgeford	..	..	14 0	12 0	..	3 37	64¾	..
Stafford	2 2	17 0	15 0	12 6	3 15	3 45	68¼	1 14
Penkridge	..	..	16 0	13 6	..	4 6	73½	..
Spread Eagle	..	..	16 6	14 0	..	4 15	76	..
Four Ashes	..	..	16 6	14 0	..	4 19	77½	..
W'hampton	2 10	21 0	19 0	15 0	4 0	4 36	83¼	1 19
Willenhall	..	..	19 0	15 6	..	4 50	85¼	..
James's Bridge	..	..	19 6	16 0	..	4 56	87¼	..
Bescot Bridge	..	..	19 6	16 0	..	4 59	88	..
Newton Road	..	..	21 0	16 6	..	5 9	90¾	..
Perry Barr	..	..	21 0	17 0	..	5 19	94	..
Birming.	3 0	23 0	21 0	17 0	4 35	5 30	97¼	2 0

Departures.

FROM LIVERPOOL AND MANCHESTER TO BIRMINGHAM.

3 A.M.	First, joins London Train at	8 30 A.M.
6 30 A.M.	Mixed	12 30 P.M.
9 15 A.M.	1st Class	2 30 P.M.
11 30 A.M.	1st Class	4 30 P.M.
4 30 P.M.	Mixed	
6 P.M.	1st Class	11 30 P.M.

FROM BIRMINGHAM TO LIVERPOOL AND MANCHESTER.

3 A.M.	First	2 30 P.M.	1st Class
6 A.M.	Mixed Train	4 P.M.	Mixed
11 30 A.M.	1st Class	5 P.M.	1st. Class

The 3 A.M. Train from Liverpool starts from the Station, Edge Hill, to which place any Passenger wishing to go by this Train must proceed to take his place.

On Sundays.

FROM LIVERPOOL AND MANCHESTER TO BIRMINGHAM.

3 A.M.	First, joins London Train at	8 30 A.M.
7 30 A.M.	Mixed	1 30 P.M.
11 30 A.M.		
6 P.M.		11 30 P.M.

FROM BIRMINGHAM TO LIVERPOOL AND MANCHESTER.

3 A.M.		11 30 A.M.	Mixed
7 30 A.M.	Mixed	5 P.M.	..

The Trains on Sundays stop at First Class Stations only.

By the Trains at 3 A.M., 9 15 A.M., 11 30 A.M. and 6 P.M. on week days, & at 3 A.M., 7 30 A.M. and 6 P.M. on Sundays

First Class Passengers, Horses, and Carriages. will, if required, be booked throughout from Liverpool and Manchester only, to London, (but not to any other place on the London and Birmingham Line for the present,) without change of Carriage at Birmingham. A certain number only can be booked by each train in this manner.

No Horses can be booked further than Birmingham, unless they belong to a Carriage or Passenger accompanying one of the abovementioned Trains.

Horses and Carriages should be at the Stations and booked at least a quarter of an hour before the time of departure.

Fares.

BETWEEN LIVERPOOL OR MANCHESTER AND BIRMINGHAM.	£. s.	FROM LIVERPOOL OR MANCHESTER TO LONDON, WHEN BOOKED THROUGHOUT AS ABOVE.
Six Inside First Class Coach	1 1	Day Trains
Second Class Closed Carriages	0 17	6 Inside Coach, G.J. 21s., London £1 10s. = £2 11s.
Third Class Open ditto by 6½ a.m. Train from Liverpool or Manchester, and by 6 a.m. Train from Birmingham	0 11	4 Inside Coach, G.J. 23s., London £1 10s. = £2 13s. Night Trains.
Passengers booked by this conveyance for the entire distance only.		6 Inside Coach, G.J. 21s., London £1 12 6. = £2 13 6
Children under Ten Years of Age Half Price. Ditto in arms, free.		4 Inside Coach, G J. 23s., London £1 12 6. = £2 15 6
One Horse	2 0	G.J. £2.. London £2 10 = £4 10
Two Horses, if one property, and in one Box	3 0	.. 3 .. 5 0 8 0
Three do. do.	4 0	.. 4 .. 6 0 10 0
Dogs, each	0 3	
Gentlemen's Carriages, four wheels	3 0	.. 3 .. 3 15 6 15
Do. do. two wheels	2 0	.. 2 .. 3 15 5 15
Passengers in Private Carriages	0 17	.. 17s. Lond. {20s. Day £1 17 / 25s. Night 2 2}
Servants	0 14	.. 14s. .. {20s. Day 1 14 / 25s. Night 1 19}
Grooms in charge of Horses, if riding with them in the box	0 14	
Servants, in attendance on their Employers, may ride outside, if there be room, by First Class Trains, at Second Class Fares	0 17	

For intermediate distances all Carriages, whether on two or four wheels, will be charged alike.

Passengers are particularly requested to see that their Luggage is safely loaded on the Carriages before starting, and that it is legibly directed with the Owner's name, address, and destination.

Officers of the Grand Junction Railway:—

JOHN MOSS, ESQ., OF LIVERPOOL, CHAIRMAN.
C. LAWRENCE, ESQ., OF LIVERPOOL, DEPUTY CHAIRMAN.
J. R. CHORLEY, ESQ., OF LIVERPOOL, TREASURER.
MR. S. EBORALL, CHIEF AGENT AT BIRMINGHAM.
MR. G. BAKER, CHIEF AGENT AT MANCHESTER.

Grand Junction Railway.—Conveyance of Merchandise.

The rates for the conveyance of Merchandise from Liverpool and Manchester to Birmingham, and from Birmingham to Liverpool and Manchester respectively, will, for the present, be as follows:—

1st Class—Heavy hardware, 1*s.* 6*d.* per cwt. No charge less than 1*s.* 6*d.*

2nd Class—Bale goods, fruit, grocery, shoes, shell fish, wines and spirits in casks, &c., &c., 2*s.* per cwt.

3rd Class—Silk goods, light trusses, toys, wines and spirits in bottles packed, fish, furniture, wool, tea, &c., &c., 2*s.* 6*d.* and 3*s.* per cwt.

4th Class—Hats, light glasses in crates, and milliner's boxes, &c. 7*s.* per cwt.

Charge for Parcels to date from Oct. 1st, 1838, between Liverpool and Manchester and Birmingham.

Under 18 lbs. weight.	*s. d.*
For any distance under 35 miles	0 6
——— above 35, and not exceeding 50 miles	1 0
Entire distance	1 6
Above 18 lbs. weight.	
For any distance under 35 miles	½d. per lb.
——— above 35, and not exceeding 50 miles	¾d.
——— 50, to the entire	1d.
From Liverpool and Manchester to London.	
15 lbs. and under	2*s* 6*d.*
Above 15 lbs.	2*d.* per lb.

Large light packages will be charged according to the bulk, &c., at the discretion of the Company. Any person sending a parcel is authorised to require its being booked in his presence, as the Company will not be answerable for any parcels that are not entered in their books.

LIVERPOOL AND MANCHESTER RAILWAY.

Travelling by the Liverpool and Manchester Railway, 1838.—The following are the Times of Departure both from Lime-street Station, Liverpool, and from Liverpool Road Station, Manchester.

First Class, 7, 9, 11, a.m., and 2, 5, 7, p.m.

Second Class, 7½, 10, 12, a.m., and 3, 5½, 7, p.m.—Stopping only at Newton, except on Tuesdays and Saturdays, when the evening Second Class Train from Manchester starts at 6, instead of 5½ o'clock.

On Sundays.

First Class, 8 a.m. and 5 p.m.—Second Class, 7 a.m. and 5½ p.m.

Fares.

	s. d.
By First Class Train—Four Inside—Royal Mail	6 6
Ditto —Six Inside—Glass Coach	6 0
By 2nd Class Train—Glass Coaches	6 0
Ditto —Open Carriages	4 6
Charge for the Conveyance of Four wheeled Carriages	20 0
Ditto Two-wheeled ditto	15 0

HORSES—For One Horse, 10s.—Two Horses, 18s.—Three Horses, 22s.

N.B.—All Horses must be embarked at the Company's Station, EDGE HILL, (Wavertree-lane,) unless accompanying Carriages to which they belong; in which case they may be embarked at LIME STREET.

Luggage.

NOTICE.—To prevent loss or mistake of Luggage, Passengers are requested to keep charge of their small Packages, by placing them under their Seats, instead of on the Roof of the Coach.—The Weight allowed for each Passenger is 60lb., beyond which a Charge will be made at the rate of 3s. per cwt.

Liverpool and Manchester to Wigan.

By the 1st Class Train 7 a.m.—2nd Class Trains 10, 12, a.m., and 5½ p.m.

On Sundays.

By the 2nd Class Trains 7 a.m., and 5½ p.m.

FARES.—From Liverpool or Manchester, 1st Class 5s.; 2nd Class 3s. 6d.

Liverpool and Manchester to Bolton.

By the 1st Class Train 9 a.m.—2nd Class Trains 7½, 12, a.m., and 5½ p.m.

On Sundays.

By the 2nd Class Trains 7 a.m., and 5½ p.m.

FARES.—From Liverpool, In. 5s. 6d., Out. 4s.; and from Manchester 2s. 6d. and 2s.

Liverpool and Manchester to St. Helens.

By the 2nd Class Trains, 7½, 10, 12, a.m., and 3, 5½, p.m.

On Sundays.

By the 2nd Class Trains 7 a.m., and 5½ p.m.

FARES.—From Liverpool, In. 2s. 6d. Out. 2s.; and from Manchester, 3s. 6d. and 2s. 6d.

Liverpool and Manchester to Runcorn Gap.

By the 2nd Class Trains 7½ a.m., and 3 p.m.

On Sundays.

By the 2nd Class Trains 7 a.m., and 5½ p.m.

FARES.—From Liverpool, In. 3s., Out. 2s. 6d.; and from Manchester 4s. and 3s.

TABLE OF FARES AND DISTANCES

From and to every Station on the Line.

Each cell gives miles / fares (first class, second class; s. d.).

BIRMINGHAM	BIRMINGHAM.	Perry Barr.	Newton Road	Bescot Bridge	James's Bridge.	Willenhall.
Perry Barr	3¼ / 1 6 1 0					
Newton Road	6½ / 1 6 1 0	3¼ / 1 6 1 0				
Bescot Bridge	9¼ / 2 0 1 6	6 / 1 6 1 0	2¾ / 1 6 1 0			
James's Bridge	10 / 2 0 1 6	6¾ / 1 6 1 0	3½ / 1 6 1 0	¾ / 1 6 1 0		
Willenhall	11¾ / 2 6 2 0	8½ / 2 0 1 6	5¼ / 1 6 1 0	2½ / 1 6 1 0	1¾ / 1 6 1 0	
WOLVERHAMPTON	14¼ / 3 0 2 6	10¾ / 2 6 1 6	7½ / 1 6 1 0	4¾ / 1 6 1 0	4 / 1 6 1 0	2¼ / 1 6 1 0
Four Ashes	20 / 4 0 3 0	16½ / 3 6 3 0	13¼ / 3 0 2 6	10½ / 2 6 2 0	9¾ / 2 6 2 0	8 / 2 0 1 6
Spread Eagle	21½ / 4 6 3 6	18 / 4 0 3 0	14¾ / 3 6 2 6	12 / 3 0 2 0	11¼ / 2 6 2 0	9½ / 2 0 1 6
Penkridge	24 / 5 0 4 0	20½ / 4 6 3 6	17¼ / 4 0 3 0	14½ / 3 6 2 6	13¾ / 3 0 2 6	12 / 3 0 2 0
STAFFORD	29¼ / 6 0 5 0	25¾ / 5 6 4 6	22½ / 5 0 4 0	19¾ / 4 6 3 6	19 / 4 6 3 6	17¼ / 4 0 3 0
Bridgeford	32½ / 7 0 5 6	29¼ / 6 0 5 0	26 / 6 0 4 6	23¼ / 5 6 4 0	22½ / 5 0 4 0	20¾ / 5 0 3 6
Norton Bridge	35 / 7 6 6 0	31½ / 6 6 5 0	28¼ / 6 0 5 0	25½ / 6 0 4 6	24¾ / 5 6 4 6	23 / 5 6 4 0
WHITMORE	43¼ / 9 6 8 0	39¾ / 8 6 7 0	36½ / 8 0 6 6	33¾ / 7 6 6 0	33 / 7 6 6 0	31¼ / 7 0 5 6
Madeley	46 / 10 0 8 6	42½ / 9 0 7 6	39¼ / 8 6 7 0	36½ / 8 0 7 0	35¾ / 7 6 6 6	34 / 7 6 6 0
Basford	51 / 12 0 10 6	47½ / 10 6 9 6	44 / 10 6 8 6	41½ / 10 0 8 6	41 / 10 0 8 0	39 / 9 6 7 6
CREWE	54 / 12 0 10 6	50½ / 10 6 9 6	47¼ / 10 6 8 6	44½ / 10 0 8 6	43¾ / 10 0 8 0	42 / 9 6 7 6
Coppenhall	56 / 12 6 10 6	52½ / 11 6 9 6	49¼ / 11 0 9 0	46½ / 10 6 9 0	45¾ / 10 0 8 6	44 / 9 6 8 0
Minshull Vernon	58¾ / 13 0 11 0	55¼ / 12 6 10 6	52 / 11 6 10 0	49¼ / 11 0 9 6	48½ / 11 0 9 0	46¾ / 10 6 8 6
Winsford	61¼ / 13 6 11 6	57¾ / 12 6 11 0	54½ / 12 0 10 6	51¾ / 11 6 10 0	51 / 11 0 9 6	49¼ / 10 6 9 6
HARTFORD*	65¾ / 14 0 12 0	62¼ / 13 6 11 6	59 / 13 0 11 0	56¼ / 12 0 10 6	55½ / 11 6 10 0	53¾ / 11 0 9 6
Acton	68¼ / 15 0 12 6	64¾ / 14 6 12 0	61½ / 14 0 11 6	58¾ / 13 6 11 0	58 / 13 0 11 0	56¼ / 12 6 10 6
Preston Brook	72¼ / 15 6 13 6	69 / 15 0 13 0	65¾ / 14 0 12 6	63 / 13 6 12 0	62¼ / 13 6 12 0	60½ / 13 0 11 6
Moore	75 / 16 0 14 0	71½ / 15 6 13 6	68¼ / 14 6 13 0	65½ / 14 0 12 6	64¾ / 13 6 12 6	63 / 13 0 12 0
WARRINGTON	78 / 17 0 14 0	74½ / 16 0 14 0	71¼ / 15 6 13 6	68½ / 15 0 13 0	67¾ / 14 6 12 6	66 / 14 0 12 6
Newton Junction	82¼ / 18 0 15 6	79¼ / 17 6 14 6	76 / 16 6 14 6	73¼ / 16 0 14 0	72½ / 15 6 13 6	70¾ / 15 6 13 6
MANCHESTER	97¼ / 21 0 17 0	94 / 21 0 17 0	90¼ / 21 0 16 6	88 / 19 6 16 0	87¼ / 19 6 16 0	85½ / 19 0 15 6
LIVERPOOL	97¼ / 21 0 17 0	94 / 21 0 17 0	90¾ / 21 0 16 6	88 / 19 6 16 0	87¼ / 19 6 16 0	85½ / 19 0 15 6

Station	WOLVERHAMPTON.	Four Ashes.	Spread Eagle.	Penkridge	STAFFORD.	Bridgeford.
Four Ashes	5¾ / 1 6 1 0					
Spread Eagle	7¼ / 1 6 1 0	1½ / 1 6 1 0				
Penkridge	9¾ / 2 6 1 6	4 / 1 6 1 0	2½ / 1 6 1 0			
STAFFORD	15 / 3 6 2 6	9¼ / 2 0 1 6	7¾ / 1 6 1 0	5¼ / 1 6 1 0		
Bridgeford	18½ / 4 6 3 0	12¾ / 2 6 2 0	11¼ / 2 6 2 0	8¾ / 2 0 1 6	3½ / 1 6 1 0	
Norton Bridge	20¾ / 5 0 3 6	15 / 3 6 2 6	13½ / 3 0 2 6	11 / 2 6 2 0	5¾ / 1 6 1 0	2¼ / 1 6 1 0
WHITMORE	29 / 6 6 5 0	23¼ / 5 0 4 6	21¾ / 4 6 4 0	19¼ / 4 0 3 6	14 / 3 0 2 6	10½ / 2 0 1 6
Madeley	31¾ / 7 0 5 6	26 / 6 0 5 0	24½ / 5 6 4 6	22 / 5 0 4 0	16¾ / 4 0 3 0	13¼ / 3 0 2 0
Basford	37 / 9 0 7 0	31 / 7 6 6 0	29 / 7 0 5 6	27 / 6 6 5 6	22 / 5 0 4 6	18 / 4 6 4 0
CREWE	39¾ / 9 0 7 0	34 / 7 6 6 0	32½ / 7 0 5 6	30 / 6 6 5 6	24¾ / 5 0 4 6	21¼ / 4 6 4 0
Coppenhall	41¾ / 9 0 7 6	36 / 7 6 7 0	34½ / 7 6 6 6	32 / 6 6 6 0	26¾ / 5 6 5 0	23¼ / 5 0 4 6
Minshull Vernon	44½ / 10 0 8 0	38¾ / 8 6 7 0	37¼ / 8 6 7 0	34¾ / 8 0 6 6	29½ / 6 6 5 6	26 / 5 6 5 0
Winsford	47 / 10 0 9 0	41¼ / 9 0 8 0	39¾ / 8 6 7 6	37¼ / 8 6 7 0	32 / 7 0 6 0	28½ / 6 6 5 0
HARTFORD*	51½ / 10 6 9 0	45¾ / 10 0 8 6	44¼ / 9 6 8 0	41¾ / 9 0 7 0	36½ / 7 6 6 6	33 / 7 0 6 0
Acton	54 / 12 0 10 0	48¼ / 10 6 9 0	46¾ / 10 0 8 6	44¼ / 9 6 8 0	39 / 8 6 7 6	35½ / 8 0 6 0
Preston Brook	58¼ / 12 6 11 0	52½ / 11 0 9 6	51 / 11 0 9 6	48½ / 10 6 9 0	43¼ / 9 6 8 0	39¾ / 8 6 7 0
Moore	60¾ / 12 6 11 6	55 / 11 6 10 6	53½ / 11 0 10 0	51 / 10 6 9 6	45¾ / 10 0 8 6	42¼ / 9 0 7 6
WARRINGTON	63¾ / 13 6 12 0	58 / 12 0 11 0	56½ / 12 0 10 6	54 / 11 6 10 0	48¾ / 10 6 9 0	45¼ / 9 6 8 0
Newton Junction	68½ / 15 0 13 0	62¾ / 14 0 12 0	61¼ / 13 6 11 6	58¾ / 13 0 11 0	53½ / 11 6 10 0	50 / 11 0 9 0
MANCHESTER	83¼ / 19 0 15 0	77½ / 16 6 14 0	76 / 16 6 14 0	73½ / 16 0 13 6	68¼ / 15 0 12 6	64¾ / 14 0 12 0
LIVERPOOL	83¼ / 19 0 15 0	72½ / 16 6 14 0	76 / 16 6 14 0	73½ / 16 0 13 6	68¼ / 15 0 12 6	64¾ / 14 0 12 0

Station	Norton Bridge.	WHITMORE.	Madeley	Basford.	CREWE.	Coppenhall.
WHITMORE	8¼ / 1 6 1 0					
Madeley	11 / 2 6 1 6	2¾ / 1 6 1 0				
Basford	16 / 4 0 3 6	8 / 2 6 2 0	5 / 1 6 1 0			
CREWE	19 / 4 0 3 6	10¾ / 2 6 2 0	8 / 1 6 1 0	3 / 1 6 1 0		
Coppenhall	21 / 4 6 4 0	12¾ / 2 6 2 0	10 / 2 0 1 6	5 / 2 0 1 6	2 / 1 6 1 0	
Minshull Vernon	23¾ / 5 6 4 6	15½ / 3 6 3 0	12¾ / 3 0 2 0	8 / 3 0 2 0	4¾ / 1 6 1 0	2¾ / 1 6 1 0
Winsford	26¼ / 6 0 5 0	18 / 4 6 3 6	15¼ / 3 0 2 6	10 / 3 0 2 6	7¼ / 1 6 1 0	5¼ / 1 6 1 0
HARTFORD*	30¾ / 6 6 5 6	22½ / 5 0 4 0	19¾ / 4 0 3 0	15 / 4 0 3 0	11¾ / 2 6 1 6	9¾ / 2 0 1 6
Acton	33¼ / 7 6 6 0	25 / 5 6 4 6	22¼ / 5 0 4 0	17 / 5 0 4 0	14¼ / 3 0 2 6	12¼ / 2 6 2 0
Preston Brook	37½ / 8 6 7 0	29¼ / 6 6 5 6	26½ / 5 6 5 0	21½ / 5 6 5 0	18½ / 4 0 3 6	16½ / 3 6 3 0
Moore	40 / 9 0 7 6	31¾ / 7 0 6 0	29 / 6 0 5 6	24 / 6 0 5 6	21 / 4 6 4 0	19 / 4 0 3 0
WARRINGTON	43 / 9 0 8 0	34¾ / 7 6 6 0	32 / 6 6 5 6	27 / 6 6 5 6	24 / 5 0 4 6	22 / 4 6 4 0
Newton Junction	47¾ / 10 6 8 6	39½ / 8 0 7 0	36¾ / 7 6 6 6	32 / 7 6 6 6	28¾ / 6 0 5 0	26¾ / 5 6 4 6
MANCHESTER	62½ / 13 6 11 6	54¼ / 12 0 10 0	51½ / 11 0 9 6	46½ / 11 0 9 6	43½ / 9 6 8 0	41½ / 9 0 7 6
LIVERPOOL	62½ / 13 6 11 6	54¼ / 12 0 10 0	51½ / 11 0 9 6	46½ / 11 0 9 6	43½ / 9 6 8 0	41½ / 9 0 7 6

Station	Minshull Vernon.	Winsford.	HARTFORD.	Acton.	Preston-Brook	Moore.
Winsford	2½ / 1 6 1 0					
HARTFORD*	7 / 1 6 1 0	4½ / 1 6 1 0				
Acton	9½ / 2 0 1 6	7 / 1 6 1 0	2½ / 1 6 1 0			
Preston Brook	13¾ / 3 0 2 6	11¼ / 2 6 2 0	6¾ / 1 6 1 0	4¼ / 1 6 1 0		
Moore	16¼ / 3 6 3 0	13¾ / 3 0 2 6	9¼ / 2 0 1 6	6¾ / 1 6 1 0	2½ / 1 6 1 0	
WARRINGTON	19¼ / 4 0 3 6	16¾ / 3 6 3 0	12¼ / 2 6 2 0	9¾ / 2 0 1 6	5½ / 1 6 1 0	3 / 1 6 1 0
Newton Junction	24 / 5 0 4 6	21½ / 5 0 4 0	17 / 3 6 3 0	14½ / 3 0 2 6	10¼ / 2 0 1 6	7¾ / 1 6 1 0
MANCHESTER	38¾ / 8 0 7 0	36¼ / 7 6 6 6	31¾ / 7 0 6 0	29¼ / 6 0 5 6	25 / 5 6 4 6	22½ / 5 0 4 0
LIVERPOOL	38¾ / 8 0 7 0	36¼ / 7 6 6 6	31¾ / 7 0 6 0	29¼ / 6 0 5 6	25 / 5 6 4 6	22½ / 5 0 4 0

Explanation.--To find the fare and distance from one station to another--say Stafford to Wolverhampton. Find Stafford in the first column, carry your eye along the column opposite to which it is placed until you arrive under Wolverhampton placed in the slanting column, and there the fare and distance will be found.

*** The figures at the top of each square denote the distance, those on the left hand the fare by the *first* class carriages, (*whether in first class or mixed trains*) and those on the right hand the fare by the *second* class carriages.

[*Entered at Stationers' Hall.*]

* The Fares from the Stations above Hartford, to the Stations on the Manchester and Liverpool Line, are the same as to Manchester or Liverpool. But the Fares from Hartford, Acton, Preston Brook, Moore, and Warrington, to the Stations on the Manchester and Live

BESC

Conveyance.—A light Va
conveyance of passengers.

WOL

Conveyances.—Two Omn
Coaches to Shrewsbury, throu
Hotel:—Royal Mail, 7½ a.m.; Sw
Wonder, 7¼ p.m. To Shrewsbur
3¼ p.m., through Shiffnal, Made
the Railway Station:—An Omni
To Dudley:—6¾ a.m.; *1½ p.m.;
Marked thus (

S

Conveyances.—Omnibus
any part of the town. Coaches
12½ p.m. Rugeley and Lichfie
Stone and Potteries, 7 p.m.

W

Conveyances.—Coaches d
A Coach through Newcastle to t
and Green's Omnibuses daily to

BASFORD AND

Conveyances.—Conveya
passengers and goods to Newcast

Conveyances.—A Coach
Sandbach, to Crewe Station, twic
Omnibus from Nantwich to Crew
gers to Nantwich.

Conveyances.—Adams' C
and Knutsford, morning and ev
From Chester there are Coaches

PRE

Conveyances.—Leaves W
noon, to meet the Trains, and ret

WA

Conveyances.—Omnibus
any part of the town. Chaises,
notice. Coaches to Macclesfiel
and all parts of the North.

REGULATIONS OF THE GRAND JUNCTION RAILWAY COMPANY.

TIME OF DEPARTURE.—The doors of the Booking Office are closed precisely at the time appointed for starting, after which no passenger can be admitted.

BOOKING.—There are no Booking Places, except at the Company's Offices at the respective Stations. Each Booking Ticket for the First Class Trains is numbered to correspond with the seat taken. The places by the mixed Trains are not numbered.

LUGGAGE.—Each Passenger's Luggage will, as far as practicable, be placed on the roof of the coach in which he has taken his place; carpet bags and small luggage may be placed underneath the seat opposite to that which the owner occupies. No charge for *bona fide* luggage belonging to the passenger under 100lb. weight; above that weight, a charge is made at the rate of 1d. per lb. for the whole distance. No kind of merchandise allowed to be taken as luggage. The attention of travellers is requested to the legal notice exhibited at the different stations, respecting the limitation of the Company's liabilities to the loss or damage of luggage. All passengers by Railway will do well to have their luggage distinctly marked with their names and destination.

GENTLEMEN'S CARRIAGES AND HORSES.—Gentlemen's carriages and horses must be at the Stations at least a quarter of an hour before the time of departure. A supply of trucks are kept at all the *principal* Stations on the line; but to prevent disappointment it is recommended that previous notice should be given, when practicable, at the Station where they may be required. No charge for landing or embarking carriages or horses on any part of the line.

ROAD STATIONS.—Passengers intending to join the Trains at any of the stopping places are desired to be in good time, as the train will leave each Station as soon as ready, without reference to the time stated in the tables, the main object being to perform the whole journey as expeditiously as possible. Passengers will be booked only conditionally upon there being room on the arrival of the Trains, and they will have the preference of seats in the order in which they are booked. No persons are booked after the arrival of the Train.—All persons are requested to get into and alight from the coaches *invariably on the left side*, as the only certain means of preventing accidents from Trains passing in an opposite direction.

CONDUCTORS, GUARDS, AND PORTERS.—Every Train is provided with Guards, and a Conductor, who is responsible for the order and regularity of the journey. The Company's Porters will load and unload the luggage, and put it into or upon any omnibus or other carriage at any of the Stations. No fees or gratuities allowed to be received by the Conductors, Gu
service of the Company.

SMOKING, SELLING OF LIQ
the Station-houses, or in any o
the passengers. A substantial
house at Birmingham, by part
person is allowed to sell liquors
—The Company earnestly hop
them in enforcing this regulati
a cause of delay, and will great

Goods sent to Birmingham,
ing Trains, are generally deliv

THE

VISITER'S GUIDE

TO

BIRMINGHAM,* LIVERPOOL, AND MANCHESTER.

BIRMINGHAM.

PUBLIC BUILDINGS.

The Town Hall,† situate at the top of New-street; open to strangers.

The Free School, New-street.

Market Hall, High-street.

Royal School of Medicine and Surgery, Paradise-street, opposite the Town Hall, where an extensive Museum is at all times open to the public.

The Society of Arts, New-street. Exhibition of Paintings open in the Autumn.

Nelson's Monument, High-street.

The Theatre Royal, New-street.

News Rooms, Bennett's Hill.

Public Office, Moor-street.

PUBLIC INSTITUTIONS.

Post Office, situate at the bottom of Bennett's Hill.

Stamp Office, Colmore Row.

Assay Office, Cannon-street.

The Cemetery, Hockley.

Proof House, Banbury-street.

* For a detailed account of objects worthy the traveller's notice, see the "Picture of Birmingham," published by J. Drake, 52, New-street; W. Wood, 78, High street; and to be had of all booksellers.

† A correct view of the Town Hall, Free Grammar School, and Market Hall, to be had on a sheet, for one shilling, at J. Drake's, 52, New-street, and of all booksellers.

H

LITERARY AND SCIENTIFIC INSTITUTIONS.

The Society of Arts, New-street. Exhibition of Paintings open in the Autumn.

Philosophical Institution, Cannon-street.

Mechanic's Institution, Cannon-street.

Botanical & Horticultural Society. The Gardens are at Edgbaston. Strangers are admitted by a subscriber's order.

Old Library, Union-street.

New Library, Temple Row West.

Law Library, Waterloo-street.

Medical Library, at the Royal School of Medicine, Paradise-street.

PUBLIC AMUSEMENTS.

Theatre Royal, New-street.

Ryan's Amphitheatre, Bradford-street.

Billiard Rooms, Waterloo-street, adjoining the News Room; New-street, adjoining the Theatre; and Cannon-street.

PUBLIC CHARITIES.

General Hospital, Summer Lane.

Dispensary, Union-street.

Asylum, (for Destitute Children,) near to Aston Park.

Workhouse, Lichfield-street.

Magdalen Asylum and Chapel, Islington.

Infirmary for Diseases of the Eye, Cannon-street.

SCHOOLS.

Free Grammar School, New-street.

Blue Coat School, east side of St. Philip's Church Yard.

Infant Schools, Ann-street and Cherry-street.

National Schools, Pinfold-street.

Lancasterian School, Severn-street.

Protestant Dissenters' Charity School, for females, Park-street.

Deaf and Dumb Institution, Edgbaston.

MISCELLANEOUS.

Barracks, Great Brook-street, Ashted.

Court of Requests, High-street.

Duddeston Hall Lunatic Asylum, Duddeston.

Old Gas Works, Broad-street.

The Baths, (swimming, and hot and cold private Baths,) at Lady Well, near the bottom of Worcester-street.

Vauxhall Gardens, Ashted.

PLACES OF WORSHIP.

Church of England.

Churches and Chapels.	Ministers, with their Residences.	Services commence.
St. Martin's, Bull-ring,	Rev. T. Moseley, M.A., Bath-row, Rector; Rev. M. W. Foye, A. M., Exeter-row, Curate; Rev. C. Arnold, A. M., Sandpits, Lecturer.	$\frac{1}{2}$ past 10, 3, $\frac{1}{2}$ past 6.
St. Philip's, Temple-row,	Rev. L. Gardner, D. D., Rectory, Rector; Rev. J. W. Downes, M.A., Colmore-row, Lecturer; Rev. B. Spurrell, M.A. 36, St. Paul's-square, Curate.	$\frac{1}{2}$ past 10, $\frac{1}{4}$ past 3.
St. George's, St. George's,	Rev. John Garbett, M. A., Hockley-hill, Rector; Rev. Layton Irwen, Gt. Hampton-street, Curate.	$\frac{1}{4}$ before 11, $\frac{1}{2}$ past 3, and $\frac{1}{2}$ past 6; Wednesday, $\frac{1}{4}$ past 7.
St. Thomas's, Holloway-head,	Rev. Wm. Marsh, M.A., Hagley-row, Rector; Rev. Charles Lowe, B.A., Bedford-place, Bristol-road, Curate.	$\frac{1}{2}$ past 10, 3, and $\frac{1}{2}$ past 6; Tuesday, 7, prayer meeting; Sunday, 7; Friday, $\frac{1}{2}$ past 7.
All Saints', Hockley,	Rev. S. F. Morgan, M.A., Grosvenor-row, Birmingham-heath, Rector.	$\frac{1}{2}$ past 10, 3.
Christ Church, Paradise-street,	Rev. J. G. Breay, B.A., Crescent, Minister; Rev. Daniel Ledsam, B.A., Summer-hill, Curate.	$\frac{1}{2}$ past 10, $\frac{1}{2}$ past 6; Thursday, 7.
St. Bartholomew's, Bartholomew-square,	Rev. Thomas Nunns, M. A., Crescent, Minister.	11, $\frac{1}{2}$ past 6.

Church of England—continued.

Churches and Chapels.	Ministers, with their Residences.	Services commence.
St. Mary's, St. Mary's square,	Rev. J. C. Barratt, M. A., St. Mary's-row, Minister; Rev. E. Hall, M.A., Summer-hill, Curate.	½ past 10, 3, ½ past 6.
St. Paul's, St. Paul's square,	Rev. Rann Kennedy, M. A., The Hollies, Hall Green, Minister; Rev. William Wenman, St. Paul's-square, Curate.	¼ before 11, ½ past 6.
St. Peter's, Dale-end,	Rev. Charles Craven, M. A., Edgbaston, Minister.	11, ½ past 6.
Bishop Ryder's, Stafford-street,		
St. John's, Deritend,	Rev. E. Palmer, High-gate, Minister; Rev. J. Collisson, B. A., Camphill, Curate.	11, ½ past 6.
St. James's, Ashted,	Rev. Josiah Allport, Ashted, Minister.	½ past 10, ½ past 6.
Trinity, Bordesley,	Rev. S. Crane, B. A., Bordesley, Minister.	½ past 10, ½ past 3; in winter 3.
Aston Church, Aston,	Rev. G. O. Fenwicke, M. A., Vicarage, Vicar; Rev. Horace Chavasse, Curate.	11, 3.
Edgbaston Church, Edgbaston,	Rev. Charles Pixell, M. A., Vicarage, Vicar.	11, ½ past 3.
St. George's, Calthorpe-street, Edgbaston,		
Handsworth Church, Handsworth	Rev. John Hargreaves, M. A., Rectory, Rector; Rev. D. N. Walton, M. A., Heathfield-lane, Curate.	11, 3.
Magdalen Chapel, Islington,		

Dissenters.

Chapels and Meeting Houses.	Ministers, and their Residences.	Services commence.
	Association Methodists.	
Newhall-street,	Mr. J. Handley, Minister.	½ past 10, 6; Wednesday, ¼ past 7
	Baptists.	
Cannon-street,	Rev. T. Swann, Wheeley's Lane, Edgbaston.	½ past 10, 3, and ½ past 6; Monday and Thursday, ½ past 7.
Bond-street,	Rev. T. Morgan, Regent-place, Harper's-hill.	½ past 10, ½ past 6; Monday and Wednesday, ½ past 7.
Graham-street,	Rev. J. Hoby, D.D., Camden-hill.	½ past 10, ½ past 6; Monday and Wednesday, ½ past 7.
Newhall-street,	Rev. J. Ham, Bath-street.	½ past 10, 3, and ½ past 6; Monday and Wednesday, ½ past 7.
Lombard street,	Rev. G. Cheatle, Lombard-street.	11, 3, and ½ past 6; Monday and Wednesday, ½ past 7.
	Calvinists.	
Bartholomew-street,	Rev. Mr. Telford, Bordesley-place.	½ past 10, 6; Monday and Wednesday, ½ past 7.
Zoah Chapel, Cambridge-street,	Rev. James Jay.	½ past 10, and ½ past 6; Wednesday, ½ past 7.
Lawrence-street,	Rev. Thomas Buckingham.	½ past 10, 3, and half past 6; Monday and Thursday, ½ past 7

Dissenters—continued.

Chapels and Meeting Houses.	Ministers, with their Residences.	Services commence.
	Dependent Methodists.	
Buck-street,	Various Preachers.	½ past 10, 2, & 6; Tuesday, ½ past 7; Thursday, 8.
	Holy Catholic & Apostolic Church.	
Newhall-street,	Mr. Barclay,	6, 10, 2, ¼ before 4, 5, ½ past 6; also daily, 6, and 5.
	Independents.	
Carr's lane,	Rev. J. A. James, Edgbaston.	½ past 10, ½ past 6; Monday and Wednesday, ¼ past 7.
Steelhouse-lane,	Rev. T. East, Sparkbrook.	11, ½ past 6; Monday and Wednesday, ¼ past 7.
Livery-street,	Rev. J. Allsop, 7, Newhall-hill.	¼ before 11, ½ past 6; Monday and Thursday, ¼ past 7.
Legge-street,	Messrs. Clay and Derrington, alternate Preachers.	½ past 10, ½ past 6; Tuesday & Thursday, ½ past 7.
Great Barr-street,	Various Preachers.	½ past 10, ½ past 6.
Union Chapel, Handsworth,	Rev. J. Hammond, Union Row, Handsworth.	11, 3, and ½ past 6.
Saltley, near the Railway,	Various Preachers.	½ past 10, and 3.

Dissenters—continued.

Chapels and Meeting Houses.	Ministers, with their Residences.	Services commence.
	Jews' Synagogue.	
Severn-street,	Rev. Mr. Chapman, Smallbrook-street, Reader.	On Saturday at ½ past 8, during the winter months, & 8, Summer months; 1, and at sunset.
	Lady Huntingdon's.	
King-street,	Rev. John Jones, Bristol Road.	½ past 10, 3, & ½ past 6; Monday, Wednesday, and Friday, ½ past 7. A Welsh service at 2 every Sunday afternoon.
	New Jerusalem Church.	
Summer Lane,	Rev. E. Madeley, Summer-lane.	¼ before 11, & ½ past 6.
	New Connexion Methodists.	
Oxford-street,	Rev. J. Curtis, Ravenhurst-street.	½ past 10, ½ past 2, & 6; Tuesday & Friday, ½ past 7.
	Primitive Methodists.	
Inge-street,	Various Preachers.	11, 6; Tuesday, 7.
Bordesley-street,	Various Preachers.	11, 3, & 6; Wednesday 7.

Dissenters—continued.

Chapels and Meeting Houses.	Ministers, with their Residences.	Services commence.
	Roman Catholics.	
St. Chad's, Shadwell-street,	Rev. E. Peach and Rev. J. Abbott.	$\frac{1}{4}$ past 8, $\frac{1}{2}$ past 9, $\frac{1}{2}$ past 10, $\frac{1}{2}$ past 3, and $\frac{1}{2}$ past 6.
St. Peter's, St. Peter's place,	Rev. T. M. McDonnell, St. Peter's place.	9, $\frac{1}{2}$ past 10, $\frac{1}{2}$ past 3, & $\frac{1}{2}$ past 6.
	Society of Friends.	
Bull-street,		10, 3, in Winter, and 6 in Summer; Wednesday, 10.
	Scotch Church.	
Broad-street,	Rev. Robert Wallace, M.A., No. 1, Summer-hill Terrace, Sandpits.	11 & $\frac{1}{2}$ past 6.
	Unitarians.	
Old Meeting-house, Grub-street.	Rev. Hugh Hutton, Edgbaston.	11 & $\frac{1}{2}$ past 6.
New Meeting-house, Moor street.	Rev. John Kentish, Bourn-brook, Bristol-road; Rev. S. Bache, Frederick-street, Edgbaston.	11 & 3.
Thorp-street,	Various Preachers.	11, $\frac{1}{2}$ past 6; Wednesday, $\frac{1}{2}$ past 7.
Cambridge-street, Crescent,	Various Preachers.	11, 3.

Wesleyan Methodists.

Chapels.	Ministers, with their Residences.	Services commence.
	Birmingham West Circuit.	
Cherry-street,	Rev. G. B. McDonald, 45, Newhall-street.	½ past 10, 3, and 6; Tuesday and Thursday, ¼ past 7.
Wesley Chapel, Constitution-hill,	Rev. T. Dicken, 17, Vittoria-street.	½ past 10, 3, and ½ past 6; Tuesday, ¼ past 7.
Islington Chapel,	Rev. J. Lomas, Hagley Road.	½ past 10, ½ past 2, and 6; Wednesday, ¼ past 7.
Bristol-road,	Rev. J. P. Haswell, Wellington-road.	½ past 10, ½ past 2, and 6; Tuesday; ¼ past 7.
	Birmingham East Circuit.	
Belmont-row,	Rev. D. Walton, Belmont-row.	½ past 10, ½ past 2, and 6; Wednesday ¼ past 7.
Bradford-street,	Rev. J. Barton, Camphill.	½ past 10, ½ past 2, and 6; Wednesday, ½ past 7.
New-town Row,	Rev. W. Griffith, Jun.	½ past 10, ½ past 2, and 6; Thursday, ½ past 7.

PRINCIPAL SHOW ROOMS AND MANUFACTORIES.*

Soho, Handsworth.

BRASS FOUNDERS.

Anderton, W. and Sons, 6, Whittall-street.
Barber, J., and Green, 15, Newhall-street.
Bourn, John, 31, Lionel-street.
Docker, Thomas, and Sons, Whittall-street.
Heaton, Ralph, 70 and 71, Bath-street.
Horn, Thomas, Temple-row.
Lingham Brothers, 170, Little Hampton-street.
Messenger, Thomas, and Sons, 22, Broad-street.
Ratcliff, J. and E., St. Paul's Square.
Simcox, Pemberton, and Co., 42, Livery-street.
Smith, Timothy, and Sons, 4, Bartholomew-street.
Standley, James, 43, Staniforth-street.
Swift, James, 7, Whittall-street.
Winfield, R. W., Cambridge-street.

BRITISH PLATE MANUFACTURERS.

Brown & Ball, Paradise-street.
Evans & Askin, George-street, Sand Pits.
Merry & Co., Cherry-street.
Sturges & Son, 26, Lichfield-street.

BUTTON MANUFACTURERS.

Armfield, Edward, Newhall-street.
Aston, J., St. Paul's Square.
Bartleet, T., and Sons, 126, Great Charles-street.
Elliott, W., Frederick-street, Regent-street.
Hammond, Turner, and Sons, Snowhill.
Hardman, J., and Co., 12, Paradise-street.

* The limits of this work would not admit of a more extensive list of the manufacturers of Birmingham, which are exceedingly numerous.

Jennens and Co., Old Meeting-house-yard, Deritend.

Ledsam, Thomas, and Sons, 10, Great Charles-street.

Smith, C. F., 14, Newhall-street.

Steadman, R., Jun., 35, Edmund-street.

CUT AND PLAIN GLASS MANUFACTURERS.

Bedford, Sarah, & Co., 16, New-street.

Henderson, (Stainer of Glass,) New street.

Price, High-street.

Rollason, Thomas, (Manufacturer to the Royal Family,) Steel-house Lane.

Osler, F. & C., Broad street.

GLASS WORKS.

Bacchus and Green, Union Glass Works, Dartmouth-street.

Gammon, W. & Co., Belmont Glass Works, Great Brook-street.

Goold & Co., Ætna Glass Works, Broad-street.

Harris, Rice, Islington Glass Works, Sheepcote-street, Broad-street.

Thomson and Shaw, Bagot-street.

GUN AND PISTOL MAKERS.

Busby, J., 30½, New-street.

Dugard, R., 29, Whittall-street.

Jones, Charles, 16, Whittall-street.

Meredith, H., and Son, 48, St. Paul's Square.

Powell, W., 49, High-street.

Pritchard, W., 135, New-street.

Redfern, B., Caroline-street.

Richards, Westley, 82, High-street.

Sargant and Son, 74, Edmund-street.

Wheeler, R., and Son, 27, Snow-hill.

HOTHOUSE AND HORTICULTURAL BUILDING CONSTRUCTORS—METALLIC AND COPPER SASH MANUFACTURERS.

Clark, Thomas, jun., 55, Lionel-street.

Daft, Thomas, & Son, Town Hall Foundry, Paradise-street.

IRON FOUNDERS.

Boulton, Watt, & Co., Soho.

Capper, Charles Henry, Broad-street.

Jones, George, Phœnix Foundry, Snowhill.

Jones, Thomas, & Sons, Bradford-street.

Mole, T. & W., Pagoda Works, Bordesley.—Show Rooms, Smithfield.

Smith, & Hawkes, Eagle Foundry, Broad-street.

JAPANNERS.

Bill, R. & G., 14, Summer Lane.

Jennens & Bettridge, (Paper Tray Makers to her Majesty,) 99, Constitution Hill.

Lane, Thomas, Great Hampton-street.

Room, James, 28, Summer Row.

JEWELLERS, SILVERSMITHS, AND EMPORIUMS FOR EVERY DESCRIPTION OF CUTLERY, PLATED WARES, &C.

Soho Plate Company, Handsworth.

Collis, G. R., Church-street.

Edwards, Ball, & Co., 82, High-street, where may be seen a very extensive stock of silver goods and jewellery.

Mapplebeck & Lowe, Bull Ring.

LAMP, CHANDELIER, CANDELABRA, LUSTRE, &C., MANUFACTURERS.

Aspinall, T., 33, Lower Temple-street.

Blakeway, John, Edgbaston-street.

Blakeway, Thomas William, Broad-street.

Messenger, Thomas, & Sons, Broad-street.

Osler, Follett, Broad-street, Islington.

Phipson & Evans, Newhall-street.

Ratcliff, John & Charles, 140, Suffolk-street.

Salt, Thomas Clutton, 17 & 18, Edmund-street.

Smith, Timothy, & Sons, 4, Bartholomew-street.

METAL ROLLERS.

Cooke, Roome, & Harley, Fazeley-street.

Muntz, George Frederick, Water-street.

Phipson, William, Fazeley-street.

Union Rolling Mills, Cambridge-street.

PIN MAKERS.

Phipson, T., & Sons, Broad-street.
Latham & Kilmister, Lancaster-street.

PLATERS, AND MANUFACTURERS OF SILVER AND PLATED WARES.

Baker, W. T., 42, Paradise-street.
Collis, G. R., Church-street.
Dixon, Matthew, 137, Snow-hill.
Kirkham, T., 13, Cherry-street, Union-street.
Parker, J., & Sons, 23½, Summer-row.
Parker, John Frederick, 72, High-street.
Ryland, William, 167, Great Charles-street.
Soho Plate Company, Soho.
Spooner, Painter, & Co., 12, New Market-street, Great Charles-street.
Waterhouse & Son, 22, Hill-street.
Wilkinson, Thomas, & Co., 15, Great Hampton-street.
Willmore & Co., Bread-street.

STEAM ENGINE MANUFACTURERS.

Boulton & Watt, Soho, Handsworth.
Capper, C. H., Broad-street.
Donaldson & Glasgow, 53, Suffolk-street.
Smith & Hawkes, Eagle Foundry, Broad-street.
Jones, George, Phœnix Foundry, Snow-hill and Lionel-street.
Penn, Samuel, Great Lister-street Steam Mill.
Tongue, W., 95, Bordesley-street.

SCREW MANUFACTURERS.

James, J., Bradford-street.
Ledsam, Messrs., Edmund-street.
Ryland, H., Oozell-street, Broad-street.

MISCELLANEOUS MANUFACTURERS, &c.

Knight, Henry, Machinist, 15, Ann-street.
Middlemore, —, Holloway-head, Saddlers' Ironmonger.
Room, W. & F., Parade, Wholesale Saddlers and Bridle Makers.
Rodgers & Co., Broad-street, Brace and Belt Manufacturers.

POST OFFICE, BENNETT'S HILL.

The following Statement shows the time of Arrival and Departure of the various Mails.

ARRIVALS.			DEPARTURE.
4 25 A.M.	..	Bristol	9 20 P.M.
5 48 ——	..	London ..	8 50 ——
7 — ——	..	Sutton Messenger	7 15 A.M.
7 50 ——	..	Banbury ..	6 50 P.M.
10 23 ——	..	Chipping Norton	3 — ——
11 30 ——	..	First G. J. Railway	5 45 A.M.
Noon	..	Bilston Messenger	2 30 P.M.
4 30 P.M.	..	Second G. J. Railway	11 15 A.M.
4 30 ——	..	Sheffield ..	5 30 ——
5 2 ——	..	Yarmouth ..	7 45 ——
5 35 ——	..	Leamington ..	7 — ——
5 15 ——	..	Oldbury Messenger	7 15 ——
6 — ——	..	Halesowen .. Castle Bromwich Great Barr ..	7 15 ——
6 45 ——	..	*London ..	7 38 ——
6 20 ——	..	Tamworth ..	7 — ——
7 55 ——	..	Worcester ..	7 — ——
8 30 ——	..	Stourport ..	6 30 ——
8 31 ——	..	Holyhead ..	6 23 ——
8 40 ——	..	Third G. J. Railway	2 15 P.M.
11 45 ——	..	Fourth G. J. Railway	6 45 ——

A second bag for London is despatched by the midnight Mail, and arrives there in time for an afternoon delivery.

On Tuesdays and Fridays a Foreign Bag is forwarded to London by a mail which leaves Birmingham at ½ past 12 at noon.

The Letter Box closes at 6½ a.m., for the despatch of the mails to Holyhead, Yarmouth, Worcester, Leamington, and Stourport; at 8 p.m. for the despatch of the London and Bristol mails, and half an hour previous to the departure of any of the other mails.

The delivery of Letters from the office window commences at ½ past 7 a.m., with the letters brought by the Bristol and London mails. Letters by the other mails are ready for delivery in 30 minutes after their arrival until 8 p.m., at which period this

* With Foreign Letters, *via* Birmingham and Chester to Holyhead.

window is closed. At ½ past 8 p.m. it opens again for the delivery of letters brought by the Worcester, Stourport, Third Railway, and Holyhead mails, and it continues open until 10 p.m.

There are two general deliveries by letter-carriers within the town, the first commencing at ½ past 7 a.m., and the second at about a ¼ after 5 p.m., except on Sundays, when there is no afternoon delivery.

When any delay occurs in the arrival of the mails, a corresponding delay will necessarily occur in the delivery.

RECEIVING HOUSES FOR GENERAL POST OFFICE.

Mr. W. Hewitt, Grocer, Hagley-row.
Mr. E. Gunn, 1, Kenyon-street.
Mr. W. Drury, 30, Lancaster-street.
Mr. T. Ash, Druggist, Prospect-row.
Mr. J. White, 235, Bristol-street.
Miss Davies, Lower Terrace, Sand Pits.
Mrs. Wood, 172, High-street, Deritend.

HACKNEY COACH FARES.

DRAWN BY TWO HORSES. Not exceeding half a mile, 1s.—ditto one mile, 1s. 6d.—ditto one mile and a half, 2s.—ditto two miles, 2s. 6d.—ditto three miles, 3s. 6d.—ditto four miles, 5s.

DRAWN BY ONE HORSE.—Not exceeding one mile, 1s.—ditto one mile and a half, 1s. 6d.—ditto two miles, 2s.—ditto two miles and a half, 2s. 6d.—ditto three miles, 3s.—ditto three miles and a half, 3s. 6d.—ditto four miles, 4s.

Returning with the same Fare, half the foregoing charges.

TIME. Between the hours of nine in the morning and twelve at night—twenty minutes, 6d.—forty minutes, 1s.—every twenty minutes above forty, 6d., for being detained.

TIME. Between twelve at night and six in the morning—double the foregoing fares.

PENALTY. Not exceeding twenty shillings, for every offence, in case any driver shall refuse to show a list of the above fairs, if required.

BANKERS,

WITH THE HOUSES WHICH THEY DRAW UPON IN LONDON.

Taylor and Lloyds, Dale-end.	Hanburys, Taylors, & Lloyds.
Attwoods, Spooner & Co., New street.	Spooner, Attwoods & Co
J. L. Moilliet & Son, Cherry street.	Sir J. W. Lubbock & Co.

Birmingham Banking Co., Bennett's-hill.	Jones, Lloyd & Co.; & Glyn, Halifax & Co.
Birmingham Borough Bank, Bull street.	Prescott, Grote & Co.
Nat. Prov. Bank of Birm. Bennett's-hill.	Hanburys, Taylors & Lloyds.
Birm. Town & Dist. Bank, Colmore-row.	Barclay, Bevan & Co.
Birm. & Mid. Banking Co., Union-street.	Williams, Deacon & Co.
Branch Bank of England, Bennett's-hill.	

Savings' Bank, Temple-row, open on Monday and Thursday, from Twelve till Two o'clock.

INNS.

The Royal Hotel,	Temple Row,	The principal Family Houses.
New Royal ditto,	New-street,	
Stork,	Old Square,	Family & Commercial
Hen and Chickens,	New-street,	Coach, Family, and Commercial.
Swan,	High-street & New-st.	
Albion,	High-street,	
Nelson,	High-street,	
Castle,	High-street,	
Saracen's Head,	Bull-street,	
St. George's Tavern,	High-street,	
Union,	Union-street,	Chiefly Commercial.
White Hart,	Digbeth,	
George,	Digbeth,	
Woolpack,	Moor-street,	
King's Head,	Worcester-street,	

COMMERCIAL BOARDING HOUSES.

J. Jones, 12, Union Passage;
Misses E. & C. Puddicombe, (Private & Commercial,) 3, Colmore-row;
J. Smith, 72, Newhall-street.—Glover, 118, New-street.

OMNIBUS OFFICES.

High-street; Bull-street, and Snow-hill.

LIST OF NEWSPAPERS.—*July* 31, 1838.

Monday—Aris's Gazette—General and Commercial Advertising Paper, established nearly a century. Average weekly circulation, 3,250 copies.

Thursday—THE MIDLAND COUNTIES' HERALD—A general business Paper, circulated to a considerable extent, gratuitously, and containing commercial and other information, but no political discussions. The guaranteed circulation is 5,000 copies weekly.

————BIRMINGHAM ADVERTISER—Tory. Circulation, 1,750 copies weekly.

Saturday—BIRMINGHAM JOURNAL—Radical and intelligent. Circulation, 2,500 copies weekly.

CANAL CONVEYANCE.

Bird, G. R., & Son, Crescent; all parts.

Crowley, Hicklin, Batty, & Co., Crescent; all parts.

Danks, J., Broad-street; Liverpool, Manchester, Hull, and all places on the eastern coast.

Danks, J., Great Charles-street; Bristol and the West of England.

Greaves, Broad-street; Stratford-on-Avon, &c.

Pickford & Co., Fazeley-street and Worcester Wharfs; all parts of the kingdom.

Partridge, W. & Co., No. 5, Warehouse, Worcester Wharf; Worcester, Gloucester, and Bristol.

Partt, C., Jun., Crescent; Stratford-on-Avon.

Shipton & Co., Broad-street; Liverpool, Manchester, and all parts of the North of England.

Smith, Great Charles-street.

Swain & Co., Friday Bridge; Hull, the North, and Sheffield.

Sturland, Thomas, Crescent; Bristol, Liverpool, Manchester, and all parts of the North.

Southan, Worcester Wharf; Bristol and Wales.

Smith & Wilkinson, 161, Great Charles-street; Walsall.

Wheatcroft & Sons, Crescent; all parts North and East.

Whitehouse & Sons; Crescent, all parts.

Worthington & Co., Great Charles-street; Liverpool, Manchester, and all parts of the North.

WAGGON WAREHOUSES.

John Shackel, 52, Dale-end; London and all parts.

G. Swain & Co., Friday Bridge; Newcastle-upon-Tyne, Carlisle, Durham, York, Hull, &c.

Mead, 138, Moor-street; all parts.

W. Ashmore, Edgbaston-street; Bristol and the West, and all parts of Norfolk.

Jolly, Bromsgrove-street; London.

Wheatcroft & Sons, Crescent; Leeds, Sheffield, and the North, Bristol, and all parts of the West.

Haines & Co.'s Fly Vans, White Horse, Moor-street; London and Bristol.

J. Butler, 88, Coleshill-street; Staffordshire and the Potteries.

Wade & Co., Bordesley-street; Bristol and the West, Sheffield, and the North.

Red Lion, Park-street, Digbeth; London, Bristol, and all parts.

PLACES OF NOTE ADJACENT TO BIRMINGHAM.

The tourist will find the following places well deserving his attention, and to which coaches are daily passing. The figures denote the miles distant from Birmingham.

The Ruins of Kenilworth Castle, 18.
The Ruins of Dudley Castle, 9.
Warwick Castle, 20.
Guy's Cliff, near Warwick. 21.
Lichfield Cathedral, 17.
Leamington Spa, 22.
Hagley Park, 12.

LIVERPOOL.

PUBLIC AMUSEMENTS.

Theatre Royal, East Williamson Square.
Royal Amphitheatre, Great Charlotte-street.
The Liver Theatre, at the top of Church-street.
Queen's Theatre, or Circus, Christian-street.
Sans Pareil, Great Charlotte-street.

PUBLIC BUILDINGS AND OBJECTS OF ATTRACTION.

Botanical Gardens, Edge Lane; admittance by ticket, to be obtained at all the Hotels.
Custom House, Excise, Dock Office, Post Office, under the same roof, South Castle-street.
Cemetery, St. James's, top of Duke-street.
——— Necropolis, Low Hill.
Exchange, Castle-street.
House of Industry, Brownlow Hill.
Infirmary, Dover-street.
Lunatic Asylum, Brownlow Hill.
Pistol Gallery, Tarlton-street, Williamson Square.
Sessions House, situate at the West of the Exchange.
Statue of George the Third, bottom of Pembroke Place, in London Road.
Telegraph, bottom of Chapel-street. May be visited on application to Lieut. Watson, at the Office.
Town Hall, Castle-street.
Wellington Rooms, Great Orford-street.
Zoological Gardens; an order, which may be obtained at any of the respectable Hotels, will, on the payment of a shilling, admit a stranger.

BATHS.

The New Baths, West side of St. George's Dock.

Whitlaw's Vapour Baths, Renshaw-street.

Sadler's Baths, Hanover-street.

The Floating Bath, Prince's Parade.

THE DOCKS.

Clarence Dock, for steam packets.

Prince's Dock, American ships.

George's Dock, in which is moored the Floating Church, for the convenience of seamen.

The King's Dock; vessels from Virginia and other ports, laden with tobacco.

The Waterloo Dock, Victoria Dock, and Trafalgar Dock, communicate with each other.

Canning Dock; vessels from the Northern ports, and in the coasting trade.

Salt-house Dock, for ships in the Levant and Irish trade.

Duke of Bridgewater's Dock, for boats called flats, in the canal trade.

Queen's Dock, for timber ships from America and the Baltic.

Brunswick Dock, vessels laden with timber.

Graving Docks. Nos. 1, 2, and 3, communicate with the Canning Dock; Nos. 4, 5, and 6, lie between the Queen's Dock and the river; two Graving Docks are attached to the Brunswick Dock.

THE MARKETS.

St. John's Market, Great Charlotte-street.

New Fish Market, opposite St. John's Market.

The North Market, Scotland-street.

St. James's Market, Great George-street.

Islington Market, top of Shaw's Row.

Cattle Market, three miles on the London Road.

Corn Exchange, Brunswick-street.

LITERARY AND SCIENTIFIC INSTITUTIONS.

The Royal Institutions, Colquitt-street.

Philosophical and Literary Society; meetings held at the Royal Institution.
Apothecaries' Hall, Colquitt-street.
Mechanics' Institution, Mount-street.
Athenæm, Church-street.
Lyceum, Bold-street.
Apprentices' (Male and Female) Library, School Lane.
Law Library, Clarendon Buildings.
Union News Room, Duke-street.

PUBLIC CHARITIES.

Alms Houses, St. Mary's Lane.
Blue Coat Hospital, School Lane.
Blind Asylum, London Road.
Bethel Union Ship, King's Dock.
Charity Institution House, Salter-street.
Charity, (the Ladies',) for Relief of Women in Childbed.
Dispensaries; Vauxhall Road and Upper Parliament-street.
Female School of Industry, Heathfield-street.
Female Penitentiary, Crabtree Lane.
House of Recovery, Workhouse.
Infirmary, Brownlow-street.
Institution for Diseases of the Ear, Duke-street.
Infant Schools, numerous.
Lunatic Asylum, Ashton-street, Brownlow Hill.
Marine Society, Mariners' Church.
Marine Humane Society.
Mariner's Church Society, Ship in St. George's Dock.
Naval Bible Society, Mariners' Church.
Opthalmic Institution, Slater's Court.
Society for Promoting Christian Knowledge, Ranelagh-street.
Society for bettering the Condition of the Poor, Savings Bank, Bold-street.
Stranger's Friend Society.
School for the Deaf and Dumb, Wood-street.
Theatrical Fund, Theatre Royal Office.
Welsh Charitable Society, Russell Place.

PLACES OF PUBLIC WORSHIP.

Church of England—twenty-four in number; the most worthy of notice being, St. Paul's, St. Paul's Square; St. George's, Lord-street; St. Peter's, Church-street; St. Luke's, Bold-street; St. Nicholas', Chapel-street; St. Catherine's, Abercromby-square; The Blind Asylum, Duncan-street East.

Roman Catholics—St. Mary's, Lumber-street; St. Patrick's, Toxteth Park; St. Nicholas', Blake-street; St. Peter's, Seal-street; St. Anthony's, Scotland-road.

Scotch Churches—St. Andrew's Church, Rodney-street; Oldham-street Church; Scotch Baptist Church, Hunter-street; Scotch Secession Church, Mount Pleasant, and Russell-street.

Unitarians—two in number; one in Paradise-street, and one in Renshaw-street.

Independents—Bethesda, Duncan-street, London-road; Toxteth Park Chapel; Great Crosshall-street Chapel; Renshaw-street Chapel; Gloucester-street Chapel; Great George-street Chapel.

Baptists—Lime-street; Great Crosshall-street; Russell-street; Cockspur-street; Comus-street; Byrom-street.

Methodists—Leeds-street; Pitt-street; Mount Pleasant; Stanhope-street; Moss-street; London-road; and Bend's Garden Chapel.

Friends' Meeting House, Hunter-street.

Jew's Synagogue, Seel-street.

TIME OF STARTING BY THE RAILROAD.

Travelling by the *Liverpool and Manchester Railway*, 1838.—The following are the Times of Departure both from Lime-street Station, Liverpool, and from Liverpool Road Station, Manchester.

FIRST CLASS—Seven, nine, eleven, two, five, and seven o'clock.

SECOND CLASS—Quarter past seven, ten, twelve, three, half-past five, and seven o'clock, stopping only at Newton.

Except on Tuesdays and Saturdays, when the Evening Second Class Train from Manchester starts at six, instead of half-past five o'clock.

On Sundays—First Class, eight in the morning, and five in the evening.—Second Class, seven in the morning and half-past five in the evening.

FARES.

		s.	d.
By First Class Train	—Four Inside—Royal Mail ..	6	6
Ditto	—Six Inside—Glass Coach ..	5	6
By 2nd Class Train	—Glass Coaches	5	6
Ditto	—Open Carriages	4	0
Charge for the conveyance of Four-wheeled Carriages		20	0
Ditto ..	Two-wheeled ditto ..	15	0

Horses—For one horse 10*s.*—two horses 18*s.*—three horses 22*s.*

N.B.—All Horses must be embarked at the Company's Station, Edge Hill, Wavertree Lane, unless accompanying Carriages to which they belong; in which case they may be embarked at Lime-street.

LUGGAGE.

Notice.—To prevent loss or mistake of Luggage.—Passengers are requested to keep charge of their small Packages, by placing them under their seats instead of on the roof of the coach.—The weight allowed to each passenger is 60lbs., beyond which a charge will be made at the rate of 3s. per cwt.

LIVERPOOL AND MANCHESTER TO WIGAN.

By 1st Class Train, 7 a.m.—2nd Class Trains, 10, 12, a.m., 5½ p.m.

Sundays.—By the Second Class Trains, 7 a.m., and 5½ p.m.

Fares.—From Liverpool or Manchester, 1st. Class. 5s.; 2nd Class 3s. 6d.

LIVERPOOL AND MANCHESTER TO BOLTON.

By 1st Class Train, 9 a.m.—2nd Class Trains, 7¼, 12 a.m., 5½ p.m.

Sundays.—By the Second Class Trains, 7 a.m., 5½ p.m.

Fares.—From Liverpool, Inside, 5s. 6d., Outside, 4s.; and from Manchester, 2s. 6d. and 2s.

LIVERPOOL AND MANCHESTER TO ST. HELEN'S.

By the Second Class Trains, 7¼, 10, 12, a.m.; 3, and 5½, p.m.

SUNDAYS.—By the Second Class Trains, 7, a.m., and 5½, p.m.

FARES.—From Liverpool—Inside, 2s. 6d. Outside, 2s.; and from Manchester, 3s. 6d. and 2s. 6d.

LIVERPOOL AND MANCHESTER TO RUNCORN GAP.

By the Second Class Trains, 7¼, a.m., and 3, p.m.

SUNDAYS.—By the Second Class Trains, 7, a.m., and 5½, p m.

FARES.—From Liverpool—Inside, 3s. Outside, 2s. 6d.; and from Manchester, 4s. and 3s.

INNS.

Adelphi Hotel, Ranelagh-street; Albion, Ranelagh-street; Angel, Dale-street; Blue Bell, London Road; Bull, Clayton Square; Commercial, Dale-street; Castle Hotel, Clayton Square; Feathers, Clayton Square; George Inn, Dale-street; Grecian Hotel, Dale-street; King William, Williamson Square; King's Arms, Castle-street; Neptune, Clayton Square; Royal, Dale-street; Saracen's Head Inn, Dale-street; Star and Garter Tavern, Paradise-street; Union Hotel, Clayton Square; Waterloo, Ranelagh-street; Wellington, Dale-street; York, Williamson Square.

FOREIGN PACKETS.

NEW YORK, on the 1st and 16th of every month, Baring Brothers and Co.; 8th, Thomas and Joseph Sands and Co.; 16th, W. and J. Brown and Co.; and 24th, Wildes, Pickersgill, and Co.

BOSTON, on the 5th and 20th of each month during the spring and fall of the year, at other times occasionally, Maury, Latham and Co., and Baring Brothers and Co.

PHILADELPHIA, on the 8th of every month, and at stated periods, W. and J. Brown and Co.

CALCUTTA direct, the 20th of each month, W. and J. Tyrer, Old Churchyard.

RIO DE JANIERO, on the 1st and 16th of every month, W. and J. Tyrer; J. Holliwell; and Ashley Brothers.

LISBON, on the 1st of every month, J. Bibby and Co., Duke's

Place; on the 10th of every month, Vianna and Jones; and on the 20th of every month, Cotesworth and Smith.

GENOA and LEGHORN, on the 1st of every month, J. Bibby and Co., Duke's Place; and on the 16th, Vianna and Jones, Chapel-street.

GENOA and LEGHORN, a conveyance once a month, John Rothwell, 2, Liver-court, South Castle-street.

MESSINO and PALERMO, once a month, John Rothwell, 2, Liver-court, South Castle-street.

BAHIA.—A regular line of Packets sails at periods, as stated in the newspapers, Cotesworth and Smith; W. and J. Tyrer; John Holliwell; Kers, Imrie and Co., and R. Tanton.

OPORTO, every three weeks, Geo. Highfield, Oldhall-street; Thos. Martin, Salthouse Dock; and Ormerod, Heyworth, and Co., Water-street; J. Bibby and Co.

MONTE VIDEO and BUENOS AYRES.—Line of Packets to sail at stated periods, which are duly announced through the newspapers, W. and J. Tyrer, and Ashley Brothers.

HAVANNAH, on the 5th of every month punctually. Ashley Brothers.

PERNAMBUCO.—A line of Packets sails at periods which are duly announced through the newspapers, Cotesworth and Smith; W. and J. Tyrer; John Holliwell; Kers, Imrie and Co.; R. Tanton, and Geo. Highfield.

WEST COAST OF SOUTH AMERICA.—Valparaiso every six weeks; Arica, Islay, and Lima, every four months; Lima direct every twelve weeks, W. and J. Tyrer; Ashley Brothers; and James Aikin.

ST. THOMAS.—Line of Packets to sail at stated periods, which are announced through the newspapers, Kers, Imrie, and Tomlinson.

STEAM NAVIGATION.

ON THE RIVER.

EASTHAM.—The William Stanley, Sir Thomas Stanley, and Lady Stanley, five times a day.—Dodd's Chester and Eastham Packet House, 32, James-street.

RUNCORN and WESTERN POINT, a steam packet every day. Office, No. 19, Mann's Island.

RUNCORN.—The Old Quay or Mersey and Irwell Navigation Company now conduct their vessels to and from Runcorn by steam power, and speed vessels are sent daily to and from Manchester, without stoppage, with goods requiring despatch. Agent, William Guyton, Manchester Dock.

To ROCK FERRY, BIRKENHEAD, MONK'S FERRY, and WOODSIDE, packets are plying every half hour from George's Dock, Pierhead; to SEACOMBE, from the south end of the Prince's Parade; and to EGREMONT FERRY and NEW BRIGHTON, from the Pierhead, north of George's Dock Basin.

IRELAND, &c.

ARDGLASS and STRANGFORD LOUGH.—The Victoria, every Tuesday. Crozier and Co., Agents, 13, Goree Piazzas.

BELFAST. The City of Dublin Steam Packet Company sail a vessel every Wednesday. John M'Cammon, 27, Water-street.

BELFAST.—The Falcon and Corsair, every Monday and Friday. Lanktrys and Co., 30, Water-street.

CORK, &c.—The St. George Steam Packet Company's Packets sail regularly to Cork, Waterford, Dundalk, Newry, and Beaumaris; and between Dublin and Glasgow; Dublin and Bristol; Dublin and Cork; Cork and Bristol; London, Portsmouth, Plymouth, Falmouth, and Cork; London and Exeter; London and Boston; London and Stockton; Hull and Leith; Hull and Hamburgh; Hull and Rotterdam; and Lubeck and Stockholm. J. R. Pim, Agent, 21, Water-street, and Clarence Dock.

CORK.—The John M'Adam, every Thursday. J. A. and R. Forshaw, 6, Goree Piazzas.

DROGHEDA.—The Green Isle, Town of Drogheda, Fair Trader, Irishman, and Grana Uile, sail four times a week. W. Splaine, 20, Water-street.

DUBLIN.—Her Majesty's packets sail every afternoon, at five o'clock, (without reference to the time of high water,) with the mail and passengers. Captain Chappell, R.N., Agent, 33, Water-street.

DUBLIN.—The City of Dublin Steam Packet Company's vessels, the Hibernia, City of Dublin, Shamrock, Commerce, Britannia, Liffey, Leeds, Birmingham, Mersey, Nottingham, Balinasloe, Kingstown, Huskisson, City of Limerick, Athlone, Duchess of Kent, Queen Victoria, Royal William, and Royal Adelaide, sail daily. Samuel Perry, 27, Water-street.

LONDONDERRY.—The Isabella Napier sails every Tuesday, and the Robert Napier every Friday. J. R. Pim, Agent, 21, Water-street.

NEWRY.—George the Fourth. J. R. Pim, Agent, 21, Water-st.

PORT RUSH and LARNE.—The Coleraine, every Saturday. J. A. and R. Forshaw, 6, Goree Piazzas.

TO THE ISLE OF MAN, SCOTLAND, &c.

DOUGLAS.—The Queen of the Isle and the Mona's Isle sail daily during the summer, and twice a week in the winter, with the mail, goods, and passengers. Moore and Christian, Agents, 23, Redcross-street.

DOUGLAS.—The Monarch sails three times a week during the summer. T. Blackburne, 9, Dale-street.

GLASGOW.—The Unicorn, Eagle, Manchester, and Ailsa Craig sail three times a week, with goods and passengers. Martin and Co., 34, Water-street.

GLASGOW direct.—The Vulcan, City of Glasgow, and Commodore, sail each once a week. David M'Iver and Co., 34, Water-street.

DUMFRIES and WHITEHAVEN.—The Nithsdale, once a week, Robert Sproat, 20, Water-street.

NORTH WALES.

The Air, with goods and passengers, for Beaumaris, Bangor, and Carnarvon. J. R. Pim, Agent, 21, Water-street, and Clarence Dock.

The Countess of Glasgow sails from George's Dock, Pierhead, for Rhyl, Voryd, Abergele, &c., every Tuesday, Thursday, and Saturday. Joseph Humphries, 33, Water-street.

The St. Mungo and Snowdon, every Tuesday, Thursday, and Saturday, for Rhyl, Rhydland, and Abergele. St. Mungo's Office, 23, Water-street; Snowdon's Office, 33, Water-street.

The Conway Castle, every Wednesday and Saturday, during the winter months, for Conway. J. T. Raines and Co., 19, James-street.

COASTWISE.

CARLISLE and ANNAN.—The Newcastle sails every Tuesday and Thursday. H. Halton, 21, Water-street.

CARLISLE and ANNAN.—The City of Carlisle and Royal Victoria three times a week. J. D. Thomson, Agent, 13, Water-street.

LANCASTER.—The John O'Gaunt. John Hadwen, Atherton's Buildings, Dale-street.

WHITEHAVEN.—Steam packets sail three times a week during the summer months, and twice a week during the winter months, with passengers and goods. W. Dowson, Agent, 8, Goree Piazzas.

WORKINGTON and MARYPORT.—The Union sails once a week during the winter, and twice a week during the summer months. J. D. Thomson, Agent, 13, Water-street.

POST OFFICE.

Delivery of Letters.—The First Delivery commences at 8 a.m., and the Office continues open till the arrival of the London Mail, (per Grand Junction Railway,) 10 55 a.m. The letters comprised in this delivery are those of the over-night Birmingham Mail (with a bag from Manchester, and a foreign bag from London); the Holyhead and Carlisle Mails (with bags from Edinburgh and Glasgow); and the Dublin Packet.

2nd Delivery—Commences about 9 a. m., with the first Manchester Mail per Railway; bringing also bags from Rochdale, Halifax, Bradford, Leeds, and York.

3rd Delivery—Commences about 10 45 a.m., and includes the letters by the 2nd Manchester Mail per Railway, with a bag from Newton.

4th DELIVERY—Commences about 12 noon, (and continues until about 3 40 p.m.,) in which are included bags from Birmingham, Walsall, Wolverhampton, Penkridge, Stafford, Newcastle, Nantwich, Middlewich, Northwich, Preston Brook, Warrington, Eccleshall, Stone, Towcester, Northampton, London, Bristol, Exeter, Falmouth; and the letters from Portugal, North and South America, and the West Indies, are also included in this delivery.

5th DELIVERY—Commences about ¼ past 1, p. m., and includes the letters brought by the Bristol Mail.

6th DELIVERY—Commences about 4 p. m., and includes letters brought by the 3rd Manchester Mail, per Railway.

7th DELIVERY—Commences about 4 50 p. m., and includes bags from Birmingham, Wolverhampton, Stafford, Warrington, Prescot.

8th DELIVERY—Commences ten minutes past 6 p. m., with the letters by the Lancaster Mail, from Ormskirk and Maghull.

9th DELIVERY—Commences at ¼ past 7, p. m. It includes the letters of the 4th Manchester Mail, per Railway, with Bags from York and Leeds.

10th DELIVERY—Commences about 7 30 p.m. and includes bags from Birmingham, Walsall, Wolverhampton, Penkridge, Stafford, Newcastle, Nantwich, Middlewich, Northwich, Preston Brook, Warrington, and Prescot.

The Delivery closes finally at 9 p. m.; on Sundays at 8 p. m.

There are Three Deliveries within the Town by Letter Carriers, every day (except Sunday); the first delivery to commence about 8, a.m.; the second about 12; the third about 5, p.m. On Sundays, only the first, at 8, a.m.

When any delay occurs in the arrival of the Mails, a corresponding delay will, of course, occur in the delivery.

The office is closed on Sundays from 9, a.m., until 1 30, p.m., and finally at 8, p.m.

DESPATCH OF LETTERS.

The following are the hours at which the letter-box is closed for making up the several Mails, and at which each mail is despatched :—

	Box closes at.	Despatched at.
	H. M.	H M.
FIRST GRAND JUNCTION.—Bags made up for Warrington, Preston-Brook, Northwich, Middlewich, Nantwich, Congleton, Market-Drayton, Stafford, Penkridge, Wolverhampton, Walsall, and Birmingham; and on Tuesdays and Fridays a Foreign Bag to London. The postage of Foreign Letters can be paid from 5 30 to 6 a.m., and up to 9 o'clock the previous evening.	6 0 a.m.	6 20 a.m.
FIRST MANCHESTER MAIL.—Bags for Manchester, Bolton, Rochdale, Leeds, and York.	6 30 a.m.	6 50 a.m.
CHESTER MAIL.—For Neston, Parkgate, and Chester.	7 30 a.m.	8 5 a.m.
LANCASTER MAIL.—For Maghull, Ormskirk and Southport.	8 0 a.m.	8 15 a.m.
SECOND MANCHESTER MAIL.—A bag for Prescot, and (per Railway to Newton) bags for Newton, Wigan, Chorley, Preston, Lancaster, Carlisle, Glasgow, Edinburgh, and Manchester.	8 30 a.m.	8 50 a.m.
SECOND GRAND JUNCTION.—Bags for Warrington, Stafford, Wolverhampton, and Birmingham.	11 0 a.m.	11 20 a.m.
THIRD MANCHESTER MAIL.—Blackburn, Colne, Bury, and Manchester.	11 30 a.m.	11 50 a.m.
PENNY POSTS.—For Birkenhead, Upton, Seacombe, New Brighton, Crosby, Bootle, Walton, West Derby, Old Swan, Woolton, and Wavertree.	11 0 a.m.	12 45 p.m.
FOURTH MANCHESTER MAIL.—Manchester.	1 30 p.m.	1 50 p.m.
THIRD GRAND JUNCTION.—Bags for Prescot, Warrington, Preston-Brook, Northwich, Middlewich, Nantwich, Newcastle, Eccleshall, Stone, Stafford, Penkridge, Wolverhampton, Walsall, Birmingham, Towcester, Northampton, London, and Bristol; and letters for Portugal, North and South America, and the West Indies. The letters for London sent by this despatch will be included in the first delivery there the following morning.	1 45 p.m.	3 20 p.m.

CARLISLE MAIL.—For Ormskirk, Preston, Chorley, Bury, Blackburn, Haslingden, Lancaster, Westmoreland, Cumberland, and all Scotland.	4 0 p.m.	4 30 a.m.
FIFTH MANCHESTER AND THE YORK MAILS.—For Manchester, Rochdale, and the Counties of York, Lincoln, and Durham (per Railway).	4 0 p.m.	4 50 p.m.
BRISTOL MAIL.—For Chester, South Wales, and Bristol.	4 0 p.m.	5 0 p.m.
DUBLIN MAIL PACKET.—For Ireland.	4 30 p.m.	5 0 p.m.
BOLTON MAIL.—For Bolton.	4 30 p.m.	5 0 p.m.
HOLYHEAD MAIL.—For Birkenhead, New Ferry, Eastham, Chester, North Wales.	6 30 p.m.	6 0 p.m.
FOURTH GRAND JUNCTION.—Bags for Manchester, Warrington, Stafford, Wolverhampton, Birmingham, and London. The letters for London sent by this despatch will be delivered there about 11 a.m.	6 0 p.m.	6 20 p.m.

INDIA.—Letters to and from the East Indies are regularly forwarded by ships. The postage must be paid when posted.

The Rate outward is two-pence per package under three ounces, and one shilling per ounce above that weight.

Letters conveyed outward in sealed bags, are charged with 8d., *single*, if sent by ship from the port at which they are posted; but if sent from any inland town, or to another port, 1s., which must be paid when posted.

FOREIGN LETTERS.—No letters for Foreign parts, except British America, the British West India Islands, and France, can be forwarded, unless postage be first paid; in default, they are sent to the General Post Office, *London*, opened, and returned back to the writers.

FOREIGN POST DAYS, at 3 20, P.M.

For Demerara, Jamaica, and the Leeward Islands, 1st and 15th day in every month; North America and the Bahamas, the first Wednesday in every month.

For Carthagena, Mexico, Cuba, Honduras, and Havannah, 15th of every month.

For Portugal, every Friday.

For South America, La Guara, Madeira, Gibraltar, and the Mediterranean, the first day of every month.

HACKNEY COACH FARES,

Which include a reasonable quantity of Luggage.

	s.	d.
Not exceeding 1,000 yards	1	0
Exceeding 1,000 yards, and not exceeding 1,700 ..	1	6
And for each 700 yards, or any intermediate distance	0	6

CAR FARES.—Two thirds of the above Fares.

N.B.—Carriages with two horses and two wheels, or one horse and two wheels, or one horse and four wheels, are considered cars. If a coach or car be detained above ten minutes, to be allowed 6*d.* for every ten minutes detained.

	s.	d.
Coach hired by the day	18	0
Ditto by the hour, first hour	2	6
Ditto, and for every subsequent hour	1	6
Car hired by the day	12	0
Ditto by the hour, first hour	1	6
Ditto, for every subsequent hour	1	0

Double fares to be paid after Twelve o'clock at night, except on public ball nights; then at such public balls, One o'clock.

The driver has the option to be paid either time or distance.

BANKERS.

Liverpool Bankers.	*Correspondents in London.*
Moss and Co., Dale-street.	Barclay and Co.
A. Heywood, Sons and Co., Brunswick-street.	Denison and Co.
Leyland and Co., 7, King-street.	Masterman and Co.
Central Bank of England, 12, Temple-street.	Esdaile and Co.
Borough Bank, Water-street.	Glyn and Co.
Manchester and Liverpool District Banking Co., 43, Castle-street.	Smith, Payne, and Smith.
I. Barned and Co., Lord-street.	Sir C. Price, Marryatt, & Co. and Bult, Son, and Co.
Liverpool Commercial Bank, High-street.	Williams, Deacon, and Co.,
Bank of Liverpool, Water-street.	Glyn and Co.
Branch Bank of England, 55, Hanover-street.	Bank of England.

Phœnix Bank, Dale-street.	Grote, Prescott, and Co.
Commercial Bank of England, Water-street.	Barnet, Hoare, and Co.
Liverpool United Trades' Bank, South Castle-street.	Currie, Raikes, and Co., 29, Cornhill.
Albion Bank, North John-street.	Grote, Prescott, and Co.
Union Bank, Water-street.	Cunliffes and Co.
North and South Wales Bank.	Robarts and Co.
Royal Bank, Water-street.	Robarts and Co.

LIST OF NEWSPAPERS.

Monday—ALBION—Whig.

————ADVERTISER—Commercial.

Tuesday—LIVERPOOL STANDARD—Conservative.

—————————— MAIL—Conservative.

—————————— TIMES—Whig.

Wednesday—COURIER—Conservative.

—————TELEGRAPH—Whig.

Thursday—GORE'S GENERAL ADVERTISER—Commercial.

—————LIVERPOOL MAIL—Conservative.

Friday——————MERCURY—Radical.

————STANDARD—Conservative.

Saturday—MAIL—Conservative.

————CHRONICLE—Whig.

————JOURNAL—Radical.

MANCHESTER.

MANUFACTORIES.

THE great centre of the cotton manufacture, Manchester, will be an object of curiosity to the stranger on this account; and he will naturally be desirous to view some of the processes and the operations of those mighty agents, steam and machinery, which have added so much to the real wealth and glory of England.

With suitable introductions, the inquiring visiter may visit the following establishments, where he cannot fail to be astonished at the vast scale on which the staple manufactures are conducted; and the remarkable order, arrangement, and cleanliness maintained through all their departments. The immense spinning mills of Messrs. Mc.Connel & Co., Henry-street, Ancoats, will furnish to the visiter an inspection of the various processes to which the raw cotton is subjected in the course of its manufacture into *twist*, or thread for weaving.

In the large manufactory of the Oxford-road twist company, in Oxford-road, he would see the processes of weaving by means of the steam loom.

In the patent card manufactory of Mr. J. C. Dyer, Stone-street, London-road, he would observe the very curious mode of manufacturing the cards used for teasing or carding the cotton; and in the large establishments of Messrs. Sharp, Roberts, & Co., machinists and engineers, Faulkner-street, he would see the various manufactures of steam engines, both stationary and locomotive, boilers, steam looms, and every other piece of machinery required for manufacturing purposes in this part of the kingdom.

In another branch of manufacture, that of silk, which is of growing importance and extent in Manchester, the visiter would be gratified by an inspection of the silk mill of Messrs. Royle and Crompton, Great Bridgewater-street.

PUBLIC BUILDINGS, LITERARY AND SCIENTIFIC INSTITUTIONS.

The Exchange and News Room, (now undergoing alteration and extention, for which end, the Post Office, now at the back of the building, is to be removed,) is situated at the foot of Market-street. It is a semi-circular building, with stone front, and the large room contains a full length portrait of Colonel Stanley, many years member for the county.

The Town Hall, in King-street, is a fine structure, founded in 1822; by application to the porter, the stranger will obtain admittance to the hall or "large room," which is very handsomely decorated with fresco paintings, and by rich mouldings, friezes, from the Elgin marbles, &c.

The Royal Institution in Mosley-street is open twice every year, during the exhibitions of paintings; one being limited to those of old masters and deceased artists; the other restricted to those of modern and living artists. The entrance hall and sculpture gallery are worth notice. Admission a shilling.

Nearly adjoining, at the back of the Royal Institution, is the Manchester Athenæum, now in process of erection, the members of which at present occupy the lower wing of the Royal Institution, with an entrance in Bond-street. The front of the Athenæum is also in Bond-street, and when it is finished the two buildings will form a very pleasing proof of the architectural resources of Mr. Barry, the architect of the two new houses of parliament.

The Manchester Mechanics' Institution is a spacious brick edifice in Cooper-street, with large lecture theatre, good library, and commodious class rooms. To the Athenæum and the Mechanics' Institution there is no difficulty of access.

The Literary and Philosophical Society of Manchester, one of the oldest and most celebrated of provincial institutions, having been founded in 1781, has distinguished itself by its annual volumes of published memoirs, and is now distinguished in the person of its President, the venerable Dr. Dalton. Its Hall is in George-street, nearly opposite St. James's Church; but as the sittings of the society are not daily, little information can be given as to the admission of strangers. Scientific men would doubtless find no difficulty in obtaining an introduction.

The Museum and Hall of the Natural History Society, in Peter-street, can only be entered on presenting an order from a subscriber. The Museum is very rich in almost every description of natural history; we believe in ornithology it is particularly so; its collection of British birds is said to be unequalled, and its entomological department is becoming exceedingly extensive.

The Concert Hall, at the top of Lower Mosley-street, is an elegant building, especially in the interior; having a neat stone front.

In Mosley-street are the Assembly and Billiard Rooms, with a plain and somewhat dingy exterior; but the Ball Rooms are spacious and elegant.

Opposite is the Portico, so called from its large Ionic portico fronting the street,—a Subscription Library and News Room.—There are two other Subscription Libraries in the upper floors of the Exchange, and a fourth in Newall's Buildings, Market street, all of considerable extent.

In an old low building, (north of the Collegiate Church) to which entrance is had by a small gate adjoining the Palatine Buildings, Hunt's Bank, the stranger will find what will amply repay even a hurried and hasty visit. This building is named the College; in it are educated a number of boys who, from their dress, are distinguished as the Blue Coat Boys. In the upper floor of the building is a long corridor, traversing three sides of the building, two of which are converted into a library, the books generally being deposited in bays, or enclosed recesses, and locked up. This library, which contains upwards of 20,000 volumes, was founded by Humphrey Cheetham, who lived in the 17th century, and is wholly free; but the books are not to be removed from the place. There is a spacious reading room at the further extremity of the library, where the student may take his worm-eaten folio, and seating himself in an old carved chair, may easily transport himself in fancy, two centuries back; for the room is of oak, pannelled and carved, with old tables, chairs, and other furniture corresponding to the period; and several old pictures of the founder and other worthies. In the library, above the books, are suspended various specimens of stuffed reptiles, and other objects, which are shown to the visiter by one of the blue coat boys, for a small gratuity; the chief curiosity in the exhibition being the broad Lancashire dialect, and strange mode of description, given by the little showman.

To the Botanic Garden, Old Trafford, Stretford Road, (to which omnibuses convey visiters to Market-street,) the admission is by an order from a member or subscriber; the secretary is Mr. S. E. Cottam, Brazennose-street. The garden covers 17 acres, and contains in its noble conservatories, some of the rarest and finest exotics and tropical plants to be seen in the kingdom.

The Zoological Gardens are about a mile and a half on the new Bury road, whither the stranger can be conveyed by omnibus from Market-street. One shilling procures admission to these gardens, which are as extensive as those in Surrey, covering 15 acres of ground, and, although of recent foundation, they already contain many very fine and rare animals, including a rhinoceros, elephant, lion, tigers, &c., and a very good collection of hardy plants.

PLACES OF WORSHIP.

The Collegiate Church.—The parish church of Manchester, and generally called "The Old Church" by the inhabitants, is within a short distance of the Exchange, at the foot of Market-street, whence the stranger, by passing through the Market Place and Old Millgate, will find himself at the principal gateway to the church-yard, which is always open. The church is a fine old edifice; in the choir are some curious carvings in wood; the canopies for the stalls show the taste of the artist in tracery. The altar piece is a relic of the loom,—a faded pictorial representation on tapestry, of which the colours and forms are now obscured by the touch of time. There are in the church several enclosed chapels; amongst others, one of the Earls of Derby. In the south transept, near the entrance to the registry, is the spot where, for a few short weeks, rested the remains of the gifted and hapless Malibran,—since removed to the church of Lacken, near Brussels. Passing thence to the registry, is a mural monument, in white marble, by Chantrey. Adjoining the registry is the chapter-house,—the ecclesiastical government of the parish being vested in a warden, and four fellows constitute the chapter, and who will probably be appointed dean and canons, when the see of Manchester is erected. The parish of Manchester is of great extent, including upwards of thirty townships.

Of the other churches in the town our limits admit but of a brief notice.

St. Ann's, in St. Ann's Square, is an example of the anomalies of some ancient parishes,—it forms, with its grave-yard, a parish of itself; and, we believe, though standing in the very heart of Manchester, it counts but one house in its parish.

St. Mary's, in St. Mary's Street, Deansgate, has a very fine spire, surmounted by a ball. This was the scene of a feat of one of the Woottons, the steeple climbers, who, by some simple apparatus, as ropes, climbed up the giddy height, and removed the old ball and cross, which had been damaged by lightning.

St. Paul's, in Turner-street, has no architectural pretensions, or other claims to special notice.

St. John's, St. John's Street, Deansgate, is a plain, brick edifice, once the scene of the pastoral labours of the Rev. John Clowes, a disciple of Emanuel Swedenborg.

St. James's, St. James's Street, is a brick building.

St. Peter's, at the foot of Mosley-street, a handsome stone edifice, resembling a Grecian temple.

St. Michael's, Angel-street, *St. Clement's*, Lever-street, and *St. George's*, St. George's Road, have little to tempt the stranger to visit them, for their external appearance.

St. Matthew's, Camp Field, is a very handsome stone structure, in the English style of architecture, erected in 1825; and the large area in front gives the spectator room to see its form and proportions, unimpeded by surrounding houses.

St. Andrew's, Travis-street, London-road, is a neat Gothic structure of stone, built in 1831.

All Saints', in Grosvenor-square, Chorlton-on-Medlock, was erected in 1820: it is a stone building, standing in the midst of an enclosure, in the centre of the Square.

St. Saviour's, Plymouth Grove, Chorlton-on-Medlock, is a stone edifice, which is intended to receive a tower at some future period.

In Salford, *Trinity Chapel*, Chapel-street, and *St. Stephen's*, St. Stephen's Street, have little to interest the stranger.

St. Phillip's, near the Adelphi, is a stone edifice, with a semi-circular colonnade in front, and a circular tower and dome of slender proportions, which have been compared to a pepper-box.

Christ's Church, Acton-square, beyond the Crescent, Salford, is of stone. Its minister, the Rev. Hugh Stowell, M.A., is one of the most popular preachers in the town. Not a mile beyond this, is Pendleton church,—a neat Gothic structure of stone, which from its position, is a pleasing object from many points of view for miles round.

St. George's, Hulme, is a specimen of the florid Gothic in some of its architectural decorations.

St. Luke's, Cheetham Hill, now in progress of erection, the first stone being laid in June, 1836, is another Gothic edifice, of some pretensions.

Amongst the dissenting chapels and meeting houses, those of the Methodists and Independents are the most prominent for their numbers and size. The Wesleyan Methodists have about a dozen; of which, the principal are the chapels in Oldham-street, Grosvenor-street (Chorlton-on-Medlock); and in Irwell-street, and Gravel-lane, Salford. The New Connexion Methodists have two; the Primitive Methodists, four; the Independent Methodists, two; and the Methodist Association, (the seceders under Dr. Warren,) five or six chapels in the town and suburbs.

The Independents have seven or eight large chapels; the principal ones are, that in Mosley-street, the scene of the late Rev. Dr. Mc.All's ministerial labours; that in Grosvenor-street, in which the late Rev. Mr. Roby once ministered; and one in Rusholme-road,—the last being the only one of handsome exterior.

The Particular Baptists have three chapels; the Society of Friends, a very large, neat building, with stone front, in Dickenson-street; the Scotch Church is a neat stone edifice, opposite St. Peter's Church, St. Peter's Square; the Scotch Presbyterian, or Secession Church, in Lloyd-street and Mount-street, is a plain brick building.

The Unitarians have four chapels; that in Cross-street, a large brick building, was destroyed by a mob, in what were called the "Sacheverel riots," and parliament voted £1,500 towards its re-erection. There is a small chapel in Salford, in Dawson's Croft, Greengate; a large and very handsome stone-fronted edifice in Bridge-street, Strangeways; and a beautiful and spacious structure, one of the purest specimens of the English style of architecture in the town, nearly completed, in Upper Brook-street, Chorlton-on-Medlock, for the congregation formerly worshipping in the Mosley-street chapel.

The Swedenborgians have two chapels; one in Peter-street, Manchester, the other in Bolton-street, Salford. There are seven chapels for the Welsh, of different denominations; three, severally called "Christ Church," for particular denominations of Dissenters; and the Jews have a synagogue in Halliwell-street.

PLACES OF PUBLIC AMUSEMENT.

Royal Theatre,	Fountain-street.
Queen's Theatre,	York-street.
Assembly Rooms,	Mosley-street.
Club House,	Mosley-street.
Concert Hall,	Lower Mosley-street.
Albion Club House,	King-street.
Billiard Room.	Mosley-street.

BATHS.

Public Baths, situate at the entrance of the Infirmary Walks.
Adelphi Swimming Baths, Reservoir Terrace, Salford.
Dolphin Cold Baths, Horrock Red Bank.
Medicated Vapour Bath, No. 1, Lloyd-street.
Whitlow's Vapour Baths, 35, George-street.

CHARITABLE INSTITUTIONS.

Manchester Royal Infirmary, Dispensaries, and Lunatic Asylum, Piccadilly; Salford, and Pendleton Dispensary, 19, Bank Parade.

House of Recovery, Aytown-street.
Lying-in Hospital, Stanley-street, Salford.
Sick Hospital, 16, Bond-street.
Female Penitentiary, Rusholme-road.
Institution for curing Diseases in the Eye, 35, Faulkner-street.
The Humane Society's Receiving Houses are four in number, viz., Lying-in Hospital, Stanley-street; the Ardwick and Ancoats Dispensary; the Lying-in Hospital, Salford; and the Salford and Pendleton Dispensary.
The Chorlton-on-Medlock Dispensary.
The Workhouse, Strangeways.
The Vagrant Office, ditto.
The Salford Workhouse, Green Gate.
The Pendleton Workhouse, Ford Lane.
Manchester and Salford District Provident Society, Office, 11, St. James's Square.
Besides the above, there are various sums bequeathed for purposes of charity, amounting to the annual income of upwards of £5,000.

RAILROAD.

For time of Trains starting, &c., see page 118.

HOTELS, COACHES, AND COACH OFFICES.

Buck and Hawthorn, St. Anne-street; Buck, Hanging Ditch; Bush Inn, Deans-gate; Eagle Inn, Market-street, Golden Lion, Deans-gate; Hare and Hounds, Shude Hill; Lower Turk's Head, ditto; Mosley Arms, Piccadilly; Ditto, Shude Hill; New Boar's Head, Hyde's Cross; Old Boar's Head, ditto; Palace Inn, Market-street; Peacock, ditto; Royal Hotel, corner of Mosely-street (the Mails start from here); Swan Inn, Market-street; Swan, Whitley Grove; Talbot, Market-street; White Swan, Shude Hill; Commercial, Market-street.

POST OFFICE.

The following are the intended Arrivals and Departures of the principal Mails at this Office, from the 6th of July, 1837.

	ARRIVAL. H. M.		DEPARTURE. H. M.	
London	10 45 A.M.	..	3 15 P.M.	—Principal London Mail.
	11 45 P.M. with Foreign Letters for the first Morning Delivery		6 15 P.M.	—For a second Delivery in London.
			6 15 A.M.	—for Foreign Letters on Tuesdays and Fridays.
Bristol	10 45 A.M.	..	3 15 P.M.	
Birmingham	10 45 A.M.	..	6 15 A.M.	
..	4 15 P.M.	..	11 15 A.M.	
..	7 15 P.M.	..	3 15 P.M.	
..	11 45 P.M.	..	6 15 P.M.	
Edinburgh *Glasgow* *Carlisle* *Preston*	5 25 A.M.	..	8 45 A.M.	
	3 40 P.M.	..	4 15 P.M.	
Liverpool	8 35 A.M.	..	6 50 A.M.	
..	10 35 A.M.	..	8 45 A.M.	
..	2 10 P.M.	..	1 50 P.M.	
..	3 35 P.M.	..	4 50 P.M.	
..	6 35 P.M.			
Ireland	8 40 A.M. or		2 15 P.M.	
..	10 40 A.M. According to the arrival of Packets.			
Leeds *York*	5 45 A.M.	..	9 0 A.M.	
	3 25 P.M.	..	8 0 P.M.	
Derby *Nottingham* *Leicester* By *Buxton*.	3 45 P.M.	..	9 0 A.M.	
Ditto By *Birmingham*	3 45 P.M.	..	6 15 P.M.	

GENERAL DELIVERIES AT THE OFFICE.

The first, at eight until half-past eight in the morning, includes Letters from London, Liverpool, Stafford, Wolverhampton,

Birmingham, Market Drayton, Warrington, Frodsham, Derby, Middleton, Bolton, Stockport, and Macclesfield, the greatest part of Yorkshire, Lancashire, Cambridgeshire, Herefordshire, Norfolk, Northumberland, Sunderland, and Durham.

The second, at nine until a quarter before twelve in the morning, First Liverpool, (per Railway,) includes Letters from Chester, the counties of Shropshire, Hereford, Leominster, part of North Wales, and all Ireland, Bolton, Blackburn, Bury, Burnley, Colne, Oldham, all Saddleworth, Ashton-under-Line, Audenshaw, Stalybridge, Hyde, Denton, Gee Cross, and Gorton.

The third, at eleven until a quarter to twelve in the morning, Second Liverpool, (per Railway,) Preston, Newton-in-the-Willows, Eccles and Kenyon.

The fourth, at twelve at noon, until half-past three in the afternoon, includes Letters from London, Bristol, Falmouth, the counties of Berkshire, Essex, Kent, Hants, Sussex, and Suffolk; part of North Wales, Cornwall, Devonshire, Somersetshire, Oxfordshire, Warwickshire, Northamptonshire, Bedfordshire, Cheshire, and all the West of England; Walsall, Wolverhampton; Stafford, Stone, Shiffnall, Chester, Newcastle, Lawton, Northwich, Knutsford, Middlewich, Nantwich, Preston Brook, Runcorn, Warrington, Frodsham, Penkridge, Eccleshall, Towcester, Northampton, Altringham, Didsbury, Cheadle, and Wilmslow.

The fifth, at half-past two until half-past three in the afternoon, Third Liverpool, (per Railway,) and Leigh.

The sixth, at a quarter-past four in the afternoon until nine at night, includes Letters from York, Wetherby, Leeds, Bradford, Huddersfield, Halifax, Rochdale; parts of Suffolk, Hertfordshire, Cambridgeshire, and Scotland, Derby, Ashbourn, Leek, Macclesfield, and Stockport; the counties of Bedford, Hertford, Leicester, and Northampton; Disley, Buxton, Bakewell, Matlock, Belper, Sheffield, &c.; Fourth Liverpool, (per Railway,) Carlisle, the whole of Scotland, the counties of Westmoreland and Cumberland, Ulverston, Lancaster, Preston, &c.

The seventh, at half-past seven until nine at night, Fifth Liverpool, (per Railway,) includes Letters from Birmingham, Wolverhampton, Stafford, Walsall, Shiffnall, Chester, Newcastle, Lawton, Middlewich, Northwich, Warrington, Frodsham, Preston-brook, Runcorn, Penkridge, Knutsford, Congleton, Stockport, Bolton, and Rochdale.

There are three deliveries by the carriers for the towns of Manchester and Salford, daily, at 8 30, a.m., at 12 30, p.m., and 5, p.m., except on Sundays, when there is only a morning delivery. The deliveries, of course, must be delayed, if any irregularity in the arrival of the Mails. The letter carriers are at the office from 7 to 8 30, a.m., from 12 to 12 30, p.m., and from 4 to 5, p.m.; but no letters can be delivered by them at the office, except to persons who have not been found when on their rounds.

The Office continues open for strangers from 8 in the morning until 10 at night. On Sundays, the office is closed from half-past 10 till half-past 12, and from 3 till 5.

HACKNEY COACH FARES.

DAY FARES. *These Fares are to be taken, either for time or distance, at the option of the driver.*	One Horse Coach.		Two Horse Coach.	
	s.	*d.*	*s.*	*d.*
Any distance not exceeding two thirds of a mile, or 1172 yards	1	0	1	0
Any distance exceeding two thirds of a mile, and not exceeding 1 mile, or 1760 yards	1	0	1	6
And for every succeeding third of a mile, or 586 yards	0	4	0	6
If for time, then for any time not exceeding a quarter of an hour	1	0	1	0
For every succeeding quarter of an hour	0	4	0	6
For every stoppage to take up more than once, and to set down more than twice, an additional ..	0	4	0	6
For every quarter of an hour waiting after being called	0	4	0	6

FARES FROM ST. ANN'S SQUARE.

Stockport Road—26 yards past Lees-street (left) ..	1	0	1	0
———— 50 yards past Travis-street (right)	1	0	1	6
Cheetham Hill—opposite further side Johnson-st.	1	0	1	0
————83 yards short of lane on left, near first mile stone	1	0	1	6
Oldham Road—27$\frac{2}{3}$ yards past Warwick-st. (left) ..	1	0	1	0
———— 18 yards past German-st. (right) ..	1	0	1	6

FARES FROM ST. ANN'S SQUARE.

	One Horse Coach.		Two Horse Coach.	
	s.	d.	s.	d.
Stretford Road—23½ yds. past Gaythorn-st. (right)	1	0	1	0
———— 31 yards short of Branch to New Eccles Road	1	0	1	6
Broughton Road—2 yards past end of Paradise-row	1	0	1	0
———— 3 yards short of first corner of Broughton Bridge	1	0	1	6
Bury New Road—6⅓ yards past door of Whitster's Arms	1	0	1	0
———— 14 yards short of line of building belonging to Mrs. Lomas	1	0	1	6
Pendleton Road—45½ yards short of Irwell-street	1	0	1	0
———— 4 yds. short of Black Horse door	1	0	1	6
New Eccles or Regent Road—32⅓ yds. past Collier-street, Liverpool-road	1	0	1	0
———— opposite end of New Quay Co.'s yard ..	1	0	1	6

FARES FROM PICCADILLY.

	s.	d.	s.	d.
Stockport Road—23 yards beyond Russel-street ..	1	0	1	0
———— 52 yards short of centre of new Sheffield-road	1	0	1	6
Cheetham Hill—7⅓ yds. short of toll bar on bridge	1	0	1	0
———— 37 yds. beyond York-place on left	1	0	1	6
Oldham Road—3⅓ yards beyond Arundel-street ..	1	0	1	0
———— 10 yds. beyond Hall's Place on right	1	0	1	6
Stretford Road—7⅓ yards past Briton's Protection Inn, Bridgewater-street	1	0	1	0
———— 11½ yards past end of factory next river Medlock on left	1	0	1	6
Broughton Road—25⅓ yards beyond Bell's Gates, Salford	1	0	1	0
———— 39 yds. short of Green Bk. Terrace	1	0	1	6
Bury New Road—2⅓ yards beyond Backhouse and Hyde's distillery	1	0	1	0
———— 52 yards past Nightingale-street	1	0	1	6
Pendleton Road—Opposite 1st corner of Walker's timber yard gates	1	0	1	0
———— 3½ yards past Smith-st., Salford	1	0	1	6

Every person calling a coach, and not employing it to such call, shall pay such sum as would have been due for carrying a fare from the stand to the place where the driver was called to.

Carriages drawn by one horse to carry not exceeding four persons besides the driver; and in carriages drawn by two horses, for every person above four in addition to the driver, one fourth of the whole fare.

The above fares shall be deemed a sufficient compensation for any reasonable luggage which the passengers may think fit to take.

When the fares for any carriage with two horses shall amount to four shillings or upwards, or any carriage with one horse, three shillings or upwards, it shall be at the option of the hirer to detain such carriage, to return in the same, on payment of half fare, provided it be not detained more than twenty minutes, and for which detention no additional sum shall be demanded.

NIGHT FARES.—After 12 o'clock at night, or before 6 o'clock in the morning, double the above fares are to be allowed; but when double fare for distance is charged, single fare for waiting only to be allowed; or if double fare for waiting is charged, only single fare for distance.

[*Time of standing, from nine, morning, to twelve, night.*]

Piccadilly Stand.—3 pair-horse, 20 one-horse coaches.

St. Ann's Square.—2 pair-horse, 15 one-horse coaches.

Railway Station and St. Peter's Square.—2 pair-horse, and 7 one-horse coaches, may stand at either of these places: they usually ply in Liverpool Road, at the arrivals of the railway trains, and at other times stand in St. Peter's Square.

Hunt's Bank, by the Church Steps.—2 one-horse coaches.

Tame-street, opposite the Crescent, Ancoats.—1 one-horse coach.

SALFORD.

Front of New Bailey.—Twelve coaches.

CHORLTON-ON-MEDLOCK.

All Saints' Church.—Seven coaches.

Upper Brook-street.—Four coaches.

Tuer-street, Oxford-street.—Two coaches.

BANKERS.

Manchester Bankers.	*Correspondents in London.*
Bank of England Branch Bank.	Bank of England.
Savings' Bank, Mr. Jn. Atkinson, Agent, 1, Cross-street.	
Cunliffes, Brooks, & Co., Market-street.	R. Cunliffe, jun., & Co.
Daintry, Ryle, & Co., Norfolk-street.	Whitmore, Wells, & Co.
B. Heywood & Co., St. Anne-street.	Masterman & Co.
W. Jones, Lloyds, & Co., King-street.	Jones, Lloyd, & Co.
Scholes, Tetlow, & Co., Cannon-street.	Curries & Co.
Bank of Manchester, Market-street.	Denison & Co.
Manchester & Liverpool District Bank, Spring Gardens.	Smith, Payne, & Co.
Northern and Central Bank, Crown-street.	Westminster Bank.
Union Bank, Crown-street.	Glyn & Co.
Commercial Bank of England, Mosley-street.	Masterman & Co.
Manchester & Salford Bank, King-st.	Williams, Deacon, & Co.
South Lancashire Bank, Crown-street.	Barclay & Co.

NEWSPAPERS.

There are five Newspapers in Manchester; four of them weekly, published on Saturday; and the fifth, the Guardian, published twice a week, Wednesday and Saturday. We annex their names and politics, and their circulation, as deduced from the stamp return for the three months ending 1st March, 1838:—

GUARDIAN, Whig	5050
ADVERTISER, Ultra Radical	3412
TIMES, Moderate Radical	2529
COURIER, Conservative	2824
CHRONICLE, Conservative	1382

*** For further particulars we refer the Stranger to the Manchester Directory.

PRINCIPAL TOWNS NEAR MANCHESTER.

Altringham. Its chief manufactures are yarn, cotton, and worsted. Population, 2,302. 8 miles S.W. of Manchester.

Ashton. Woollens. Population, 9,222. 7 miles E.

Bolton. Muslin, quilting, and dimity. Population, 22,037. 11 miles N.W.

Bury. Cotton. Population, 10,583. 9 miles N.N.W.

Fairfield. A Moravian settlement. 4 miles E.

Knutsford. Thread, worsted, and leather. Population, 2,753. 15 miles S.

Macclesfield. Silk. Population, 17,746. 18 miles S.

Middleton. Cotton. Population, 12,793. 7 miles N.

Newton. Fustian and cotton. Population, 1,643. 16 miles W.

Rochdale. Woollen and strong cotton goods. Population, 61,011. 12 miles N.

Stockport. Cotton. Population, 21,726. 7 miles S.

Warrington. Cotton. Population, 13,570. 15 miles W.

Wigan. Cotton and linen. Population, 17,716. 18 N.W.

INDEX.

BIRMINGHAM:—Printed by James Drake, 52, New-street.

EDWARDS, BALL AND CO.,

82, High-street, Birmingham,

JEWELLERS, SILVERSMITHS, CUTLERS, &c.,

EMPORIUM

FOR THE MANUFACTURES OF

BIRMINGHAM, SHEFFIELD, AND LONDON.

Established nearly a century.

THIS spacious suite of Rooms offers to the inspection of the Visiter, an extensive selection of fashionable Jewellery, Gold and Silver Plate; and a large assortment of second hand Plate; Plated Wares of every variety; Fancy Silver Goods; Gilt Jewellery and Trinkets; Gold and Silver Watches; German Silver, and Plated on Steel Articles; Warranted Cutlery, Elastic Razors, and Strops; Fancy Hearth Brushes; Papier Mâchée Trays and Japanned Wares; Bronze Tea and Coffee Urns; Britannia Metal Goods; Bronze and Or Molu Suspending and Table Lanps, Candelabra, Lustres, Inkstands, &c.; Regulation and Dress Swords; Patent Corkscrews; Snuffers and Polished Steel Articles of every description.

N.B. Canteens made and fitted to contain Plate. Livery Button Dies cut, and Buttons made to order on the shortest notice. Medals and Seals for Public Companies and Scientific Societies, Communion Services, Presentation Plate, and Silver Cups designed and executed in the first style of Art.

Arms, Crests, and Mottos Engraved.

FURNISHING IRONMONGERY IN GENERAL.

V. R.

MAPPLEBECK AND LOWE'S

EMPORIUM FOR THE MANUFACTURES OF

BIRMINGHAM, LONDON, AND SHEFFIELD

MANUFACTURING AND FURNISHING IRONMONGERY,

Wholesale and Retail.

BY APPOINTMENT,

Agents to Messrs. JOSEPH RODGERS and SONS, Sheffield, Cutlers to her Majesty.

THE Nobility, Gentry, and Strangers visiting Birmingham, are respectfully invited to this Establishment, whether as Purchasers, or Parties in search of amusement. The SHOW ROOMS, contain the finished articles for Sale that are manufactured in this Town, London, and Sheffield—and are open to all persons of respectability. Cards of admission, to inspect some of the distinguished Manufactories, may be obtained at this Establishment.

Cutlery Show Rooms,

Contains an elegant and splendid assortment of every description of articles in Cutlery, and beautiful specimens from the Manufactory and Show Rooms of Messrs. Rodgers and Sons, and various other articles which present novelties of unusual taste and variety; also, an extensive variety of rich *Sheffield Plated Wares*, (with strong Silver edges and shields for engraving arms or crests upon,) *German Silver and Britannia Metal Goods.*

Furnishing Show Room,

Contains splendid Patent Fire Places, elegant Bronzed Steel and Or-molu Stove Grates, Fenders, Fire Irons and supports.——Bronzed Tea and Coffee Urns, Kettles on Stands, &c. &c., of the best manufacture, and entirely new patterns.—A splendid assortment of the best Japanned Papier Machée Trays and Waiters; also, Ladies' Work Tables, Fire Screens, Card Racks, and Cases from the first manufacturers.——Bronzed Inkstands, Lustres, Thermometers, Card Racks, Wax Tapers, &c. &c.——Chandelier, Table, Hall, Candle and other Lamps, and Candelabras in Bronze and Or-molu.

Establishment for Furnishing

Gentlemen's Seats, Halls, Houses, &c., in the most complete manner and first style of elegance: Kitchen Ranges, on most improved principles; Economical Cooking Apparatus, with the latest improvements, and every description of Ironmongery, and superior Braizery Goods; improved Shower Baths, with Pump; Warm, Cold, Hip, and Feet Baths; Horticultural Implements in great variety, viz., Tool Chests, Fumigating Bellows, Scott's Portable Garden Pumps, Engines, and Mennogrammes (or improved Labels) for Flower Pots, &c., highly approved of by the first Horticulturists.

EXPERIENCED BELL-HANGERS AND LOCKSMITHS SENT TO ANY PART OF THE COUNTRY.

The Wholesale Ironmongery business connected with this Establishment, is conducted at No. 1, GOLDEN COURT, adjoining.

*** *Goods for Exportation and Shipping Orders, executed on the most advantageous terms.*

6, Bull Ring, Birmingham.

V. R.

JAMES BROWN,

MANUFACTURER OF

BRITANNIA METAL GOODS,

Paradise-street, Birmingham.

JOHN LILLEY, JUN.,

MANUFACTURER OF

SILVER AND PLATED WARES,

MILITARY ORNAMENTS, &c.,

OF EVERY DESCRIPTION,

23, St. Paul's Square, Birmingham.

THOMAS HORTON, AND CO.,

MAKERS OF GERMAN SILVER,

AND MANUFACTURERS OF

SPOONS, FORKS, &c.,

IN THE IMPROVED BRITISH PLATE,

34, Lench-street, Birmingham.

V.  R.

W. HOPKINS & SON,

(Late James Barron,)

PATENT BLIND

MANUFACTURERS,

AND

GENERAL BRASS FOUNDERS,

25, LOWER TEMPLE-STREET,

Birmingham.

MAPS MOUNTED ON A SUPERIOR PRINCIPLE;

SPRING BLINDS FOR SHOP FRONTS,

ON AN IMPROVED CONSTRUCTION;

GAUZE WIRE BLINDS,

OLD BLINDS PAINTED AND REPAIRED,

&c., &c., &c.

V.  R.

ROYAL HOTEL,

MAIL AND COACH OFFICE.

FROM THIS OFFICE,

DEPART ALL

HER MAJESTY'S ROYAL MAILS,

(Except the Burnley Mail);

ALSO, A GREAT NUMBER OF

FIRST-RATE,

FAST, FOUR-HORSE COACHES:

THUS AFFORDING

OPPORTUNITIES FOR TRAVELLING

By Superior Conveyances, to the

NORTH, INTO YORKSHIRE, AND TO ALL PARTS OF THE KINGDOM,

ALMOST HOURLY.

LACY AND ALLEN,

PROPRIETORS.

COMMERCIAL AND FAMILY HOUSE,

KING'S ARMS

HOTEL,

JOHN ELTON,

KING-STREET, MANCHESTER.

MARY OGDEN,

COMMERCIAL INN,

MARKET-STREET,

CORNER OF BROWN-STREET,

MANCHESTER.

V.  **R.**

JENNENS & BETTRIDGE,

Japanners and Manufacturers

OF

PAPIER MÂCHÉE, &c.

TO HER MAJESTY,

(And to their late Majesties, George and William the Fourth,)

99, CONSTITUTION HILL,

BIRMINGHAM,

AND

3, HALKIN-STREET WEST,

BELGRAVE SQUARE, LONDON.

THIS ESTABLISHMENT IS OPEN TO THE INSPECTION OF VISITERS.

N.B. Cards of Admission to the principal Manufacturing Establishments and Show Rooms in Birmingham, may be had of J. and B.

V.  R.

By Special Appointment.

T. J. MORRIS,

REPOSITORY OF ARTS,

COLMORE-ROW, BIRMINGHAM,

MANUFACTURER OF

Superfine Water Colours in Cakes,

AND

FINE HAIR PENCILS,

In Ordinary to Her Most Gracious Majesty the Queen,
Her Majesty the Queen Dowager,
and the
Duke of Sussex.

LONDON, and 28, Colmore Row, BIRMINGHAM.

Circulating Port Folios, consisting of the choicest Drawings, Flowers by Holland and Edwards, Pole and Hand Screens, Card Racks, Gold Papers and Borders, Screen Handles, White Wood-work for Painting, Ivory and British Boards, and Fancy Stationery.

Papier Machee of every description.

Materials for Chinese Japan Painting, Hollands and Harding's Colours, Brookman and Langdon's, and Banks' Lead Pencils, Drawing Materials, Varnishing in a Superor Style, Ivories for Miniatures, Prepared Canvass and Bladder Colours.

MORDAN'S EVER-POINTED PENCILS AND PEN HOLDERS.

BIRMINGHAM: Printed by James Drake, 52, New-street.